NO NONSENSE PARENTING GUIDE™

TOUGH TOPICS

D1415026

THE NO NONSENSE LIBRARY

OTHER NO NONSENSE PARENTING GUIDES

Baby Names
Fathering
Feeding Your Baby
Play and Learn
Pregnancy, Birth and Bonding
Raising a Happy Baby
Your Baby's Health and Safety
Your Growing Baby
The Working Mother

OTHER NO NONSENSE GUIDES

Car Guides
Career Guides
Cooking Guides
Financial Guides
Health Guides
Legal Guides
Real Estate Guides
Study Guides
Success Guides
Wine Guides

TOUGH TOPICS

How to Use Books in Talking
with Children About
Life Issues and Problems

SARA WILFORD

LONGMEADOW PRESS

This publication is designed to provide accurate and authoritative information regarding the subject matter covered. This text is not meant to be exhaustive on the information presented herein. Neither the publisher nor the author is engaged in providing professional services or medical advice. Should assistance be desired, the services of a competent professional should be sought.

No Nonsense Parenting Guide is a trademark controlled by Longmeadow Press.

Published by Longmeadow Press, 201 High Ridge Road, Stamford, Connecticut 06904. No part of this book may be reproduced or used in any form or by any means, electronic or mechanical, including photocopying, recording, or by an information storage and retrieval system, without permission in writing from the publisher.

ISBN: 0-681-40720-4

Printed in the United States of America

0 9 8 7 6 5 4 3 2 1

*For all the children, parents, and teachers
who have so enriched my personal life
and professional understandings*

ABOUT THE AUTHOR

Sara Wilford is director of Sarah Lawrence College's Early Childhood Center and Art of Teaching graduate program. College teacher, workshop leader, and former public elementary-school teacher, she has two graduate degrees from Bank Street College of Education. She is a member of the Child Growth and Development Corporation advisory board.

CONTENTS

Introduction:
THE POWER
OF BOOKS

"The bird was dead when the children found it. . . ."

An intense silence falls over the class of preschoolers. No one moves. Each child's eyes are riveted on the book.

The teacher continues to read Margaret Wise Brown's classic, *The Dead Bird*, in a voice that indicates, despite her desire to keep the tone even, that she herself is moved.

As the children in the story conclude the cycle of grief, mourning, commemoration, and return to normal pleasures, the book ends. The children in the room do not speak at first. Then Maria says:

"Mrs. Rogers died."

"She used to be our teacher." Brad looks thoughtful.

"She had an accident," Maria counters.

The teacher says, "That's right. I feel very sad." But, she doesn't go on. Children have not, until this moment, spoken of the tragedy of their former teacher's death. "Now, the feelings will emerge," she thinks. "Next week, the questions will begin to come."

* * *

I have learned a great deal from observing teachers of young children over the years. One of the most impressive images continues to be the sight of a sensitive teacher using a book as a vehicle to make contact with an individual child or an entire class. The book, carefully chosen to meet a specific situation or take on a pressing issue, becomes a powerful, yet neutral, focus for discussion. It says that the teacher understands, that the adult can be trusted to communicate honest, accurate information and take on probing questions in return.

Although "bibliotherapy" (the use of books for therapeutic purposes) is an interesting concept, it is not what I am advocating here. I'm suggesting instead that parents (along with significant others) and teachers are the most important influences in children's lives. Working together, these important people can use their own rich, individual, human skills for coping with the life issues and problems of children's early years. To do so, they need a solid understanding of how young people grow and develop and a repertoire of techniques and tools.

I hope that this book will set the stage for a partnership between parents and teachers and provide an understanding of developmental stages through which young children progress. Most of all, I hope that readers will gain a useful repertoire of techniques to use in talking with children about troublesome issues and find the books listed under tough topics to be of specific help.

Books are potent. They are agents of information. They have the power to open discussions, to create an atmosphere of empathy, and to set a scene of impartiality in which we can discover our children's thoughts.

1

PARENTS AND TEACHERS WORKING TOGETHER

Common Goals

Do parents want their children to lead rewarding lives? . . . to be successful in school? . . . to make friends? It sounds silly to even ask these questions because the answer to each is obviously YES!

Do teachers want their pupils to enjoy coming to school? . . . to do their work productively, with under-standing? . . . to get along with their peers? Of course.

Parents and teachers have the same basic goals for children. They want children to:

LEAD REWARDING LIVES
ACQUIRE UNDERSTANDINGS AND
    COMPETENCIES
ENJOY FAMILY AND FRIENDS

All of this sounds wonderful, even easy. If the adults who influence children the most want the same things for them, then shouldn't everything run smoothly as children grow, enter school, and begin to mature? The hitch is that we can't predict the differences in children's development—or the things that happen to them in life over which neither we nor they have control. We have to accept the fact that the perfection we wish for is unattainable.

A more realistic view of what we want for children does not have to do with changing goals, but rather with adults working together for children's benefit. A sudden growth spurt introduces a child to new questions, fears, or temptations. Life—to borrow a term from another game of surprises—throws an unexpected "curve ball" in the form of a new baby in the family, parental separation, or perhaps the death of a loved one. There is no one to blame, but there are victims if no one intervenes. And the ones who can most effectively intervene are those who know the children best: their parents and teachers.

Parents and teachers, as collaborative partners, can be superb child advocates, but in my experience, effective collaboration takes place only when both parties understand the different perspectives from which they approach their common goals.

An assistant teacher in the early childhood center that I direct has a child in one preschool program and teaches in another. Both programs are conducted in the same room, but during different parts of the day. Recently, bursting into my office for her first conference with me, the teacher announced: "It's wild! I just walked into the same room where I taught so confidently this morning, but this afternoon I brought Jenny to school. I'm a *mom*, and I'm a nervous wreck!"

This young woman is operating from two perspectives—that of teacher and parent—but not simultaneously. Taking off from this example, let's examine both the parent's world and the teacher's world in an effort to bring them closer together.

On Wanting to Be a "Perfect Parent"

Identifying with Your Child

Wanting to be a "perfect parent" begins with the birth of your child. Your feelings during the child's early years tend to be particularly intense. Much of this has to do with a parent's own childhood memories and sense of vulnerability that are aroused through identification as each new member of the family comes along. Your baby's every developmental accomplishment brings with it a sense of pride and excitement, from the initial smile and coo to the physical landmarks of sitting, crawling, and that momentous first step. Your enthusiastic responses encourage your baby or toddler to continue to practice newly discovered skills.

If, on the other hand, development does not seem to be progressing "on schedule," you may go overboard by responding with undue anxiety. Sometimes tensions are enhanced by the competitive society in which we live. Imagine the range of emotions aroused in four-year-old Johnny's parents as they return from a disturbing conference with his teacher. She wants to "hold him back!" She says he'll never learn to read in kindergarten! In fact, the teacher may not have said these very words. She may be suggesting, instead, that the benefits of an extra year in preschool will enhance Johnny's social and emotional development. But this is not what Johnny's parents heard.

Worrying

As I've suggested, parents identify with their children. They love them. They care deeply about their children's success, and this can cause them to ask questions and make comments like the following, which reflect worry and anxiety.

> "Will my child be reading by the end of kindergarten?"
> "Why is Alex's penmanship so AWFUL!"
> "Will Annie *always* write her name backwards?"
> "You should see the way my fourth grader spells! (*Exasperated gasp.*) Must have some terrible teacher!"

If the above sounds familiar, it's because wanting your child to do well is a natural impulse. The trouble is, it's easy to forget that each child is different. We confuse the goals we hold for our kids with the idea that "the sooner they can do it, the smarter they'll be." Before you invest misplaced energy in worrying about how well your youngster is doing compared to the one next door, think about this for a minute: are all the six-year-old children you know the same size? It's obvious that they're not. Even though there are genetic differences at work, some of the smallest six-year-olds you know will eventually, and unpredictably, grow to be the tallest in their classes.

Using Your Own Knowledge

Today's parents are under a lot of pressure, both in the workplace and at home (where time is scarce and support systems are often lacking). We are beleaguered by confusing information that floods bookstores, newspapers and magazines, and the media. What are we to make of one title promising to "multiply your baby's intelligence" and another warning that early formal instruction should be labeled "miseducation"?

Perhaps we are losing touch with a great, unlearned gift—common sense. As I talk with parents of young children I am impressed by how much they know, both intuitively and through observation, about their own offspring. Sometimes this results in legitimate concerns because parents may be able to discern unusual symptoms or patterns of behavior that can be overlooked by a pediatrician or others who have only sporadic contact with a child. If they have acquired a sound understanding of child development principles, parents are able to make balanced assessments. Armed with information about the individual ways in which young children learn and trusting their own instincts, they can look at their child and say, for example:

> Paul is within the normal range of "beginning to learn to read." He has a lot of trouble holding a pencil . . . even a crayon . . . and it's going to take him some time to write legibly. *But* what stories he can tell, how he loves to hear us read aloud—and he can sort and classify a rock collection with much greater attention to detail than we can!

* * *

Major thinkers of this century, such as the Swiss psychologist Jean Piaget, have helped us understand more about how children think and learn. Current educational findings indicate that a recipe for success demands such ingredients as "enthusiasm," "venturesomeness," and "the ability to risk." Parents can feel confident when they look at their individual child's development in knowing that feelings and attitudes play as important a part in the learning process as the acquisition of information and knowledge. And child development research supports the premise that pushing children to succeed at tasks they are not yet mature enough to incorporate comfortably can produce negative results in later years.

From the Teacher's Point of View

The Futurist

Sitting at the back of a school auditorium in 1980, a public-school teacher listened to an in-service lecture given by a well-known "futurist"—a predictor of the nation's climate and temper in the years to come.

"YOU!" he exclaimed, pointing his finger at the mesmerized audience of elementary-school teachers, "YOU will be the ones to take the rap! Many changes have taken place in this country and abroad. People are afraid of what's going to happen, not only to the United States but to the world. And when people are afraid, they revert to what they know . . . to what makes them feel comfortable. They attack the very institutions whose forward-thinking practices they used to support. Schools are the most significant institutions for parents.

"Parents will want their children to learn in the narrowest, most traditional sense. And unless YOU get YOUR acts together and start telling parents why you want to teach in new and exciting ways, then YOU . . . YOU are going to be blamed for anything and everything that frightens these parents about their society!"

Perhaps the futurist went a little far. But the image he tried to implant is a valid picture of the impact societal changes can have on the teaching profession.

An Historical Perspective

What is the *best* way to teach children? If this sounds like a simple question, don't be fooled into thinking there's a simple answer. What compounds the question and its answer is the complex relationship between parents and schools. For schools are responsible to their clients, and although children are the actual clients, parents are the spokesmen for them. Looking back at education in the United States during the last half century is a little like viewing a clock pendulum swing from one extreme to the other.

The Progressive Movement

The progressive education movement swept over many parts of this country in the early 1900s, reaching its zenith in the late 1930s. Led by John Dewey, it brought a breath of fresh air to school systems whose curricula were often rigid and dry. Dewey's premise that children "learn by doing" was only a part of his thoughtful and brilliant philosophy of education, a philosophy that extended to a union of theory and practice. Rather than demanding less of teachers, it demanded more, calling for a deep under-standing of how children grow, develop, and learn.

By the 1940s, *progressive education* was a respected and accepted term, used to characterize many of our nation's schools. This was a period when Dr. Benjamin Spock was urging parents to be more relaxed and sensitive in their child-rearing practices, and psychotherapeutic principles were appreciated as important in considering the healthy development of children. However, in striving to imple-ment Dewey's theories, many schools gradually concen-trated more on the children's need to express themselves than on how and what they were learning—or on the role of the teacher in the learning process.

Sputnik!

Picture our imaginary pendulum swinging to the opposite extreme, propelled by a dramatic event—SPUTNIK! The Soviet Union launched its first satellite into space in 1957, jarring the United States into the realization that its posi-tion as "world leader" might not forever remain secure.

Just two years earlier, Rudolf Flesch had written his by now famous book, *Why Johnny Can't Read*. A conserva-tive mood descended on our schools, responsive to paren-tal panic about a shifting balance of world power and the need for our children to survive new challenges. "The old way, the way we know" seemed a safe route to take, led by a return to old-fashioned teaching methods, with parents hailing phonics as the one and only way to teach a child to read.

More Swings of the Pendulum

In the 1960s and early 1970s, the United States' educational establishment felt the effects of a powerful British reform movement. The impact of "open classroom" teaching traveled the Atlantic and was embraced by American schools—but schools that were all too often unprepared to accept its implied rigor. Organizing a classroom in which children are purposeful yet free to move about is a lot more difficult—though much more rewarding—than teaching children anchored to desks set in neat rows. Based, in large part, on Jean Piaget's theory of intellectual development, "open education" resonated with much of John Dewey's philosophy of progressive education! The excitement caused by this new infusion of child-centered teaching methods still affects us. But the pendulum has today swung once again toward a "back to basics" focus as families struggle to find safety in a search for "traditional values."

Parents and Teachers Today

As more and more teachers become researchers, we can return to the futurist and answer him squarely. Teachers *do* know more about how children learn and about how they construct meaning within the context of their lives at school. Also, they are making this information available to parents and colleagues through a host of new articles and books.

Parents feel vulnerable as they face a competitive society and an uncertain world. They may seek refuge in what they conceive of as a safe, "traditional," education for their youngsters, but they can change the pattern.

They can inform themselves about the process of child development, and they can utilize their instincts as acute observers.

These two powerful groups of people—teachers and parents—are children's greatest advocates. They can achieve mutual respect and rapport if not always consensus. By talking with one another and being open-minded about each other's points of view, parents and teachers can join together in listening and responding to children.

SUGGESTED READING

Early Schooling: The National Debate ed. by Sharon Kagan and Edward Zigler. New Haven: Yale University Press, 1988. A scholarly, up-to-date collection that should provoke discussion between parents and teachers.

The Hurried Child: Growing Up Too Fast Too Soon by David Elkind. Reading, MA: Addison-Wesley, 1981. A well-known book on the disturbing phenomenon of pressuring our children to grow up quickly—without consideration of their developmental needs.

The Learning Child by Dorothy Cohen. New York: Schocken Books, Inc., 1988. A wise and substantive book about the process of intellectual development from kindergarten through sixth grade. A classic.

Miseducation: Preschoolers at Risk by David Elkind. New York: Alfred A. Knopf, 1987. An important volume both for parents and teachers with specific information about the importance of appropriate early childhood curricula.

More Than the ABCs: The Early Stages of Reading and Writing (#204) by Judith A. Schickedanz. Washington, DC: National Association for the Education of Young Children, 1986. This fine book on the development and interrelationship of reading and writing covers infancy through the early elementary years.

On Learning to Read: The Child's Fascination with Meaning by Bruno Bettelheim and Karen Zelan. New York: Random House, 1982. A famous psychologist turns his attention to the reading process and the construction of meaning.

The Ordinary Is Extraordinary: How Children Under Three Learn by Amy L. Dumbro and Leah Wallach. New York: Simon & Schuster, 1988. This book is a great antidote for parents interested in flash cards for babies!

Reading Begins at Home by Dorothy Butler and Marie Clay. Portsmouth, NH: Heinemann Educational Books, 1987. An appropriate and extremely useful book, current in its approach to the beginnings of reading.

Teacher–Parent Relationships by Jeanette G. Stone. Washington, DC: National Association for the Education of Young Children, 1987. Particularly helpful for teachers as they prepare to talk with parents about their children.

What Did I Write? by Marie Clay. Portsmouth, NH: Heinemann Educational Books, 1975. An illustrated documentation of the gradual development of young children's writing.

2

LISTENING AND RESPONDING TO CHILDREN

Parents sometimes face questions from their children that seem difficult to answer:

> "Why can't I let that nice man drive me home from school?"
>
> "Why did Fido have to die?"
>
> "How do you *really* make a baby?"
>
> "What does AIDS mean?"

Events occur in the natural course of children's growth and development (and in the context of evolving family life), which can be unsettling along a continuum from mild to severe.

Teachers also face questions from children in their classes that may be similar to those heard by parents. In fact, teachers and child-care workers are spending more and more time with our children, as the numbers of single-parent families and families with both parents in the out-of-home work force rise daily. Teachers must concern themselves with talking about stressful school happenings, from the death of a favorite class pet to the serious illness of a classmate. They are expected to be able to understand the press of normal life events on their growing pupils, handle the special problems of handicapped youngsters, and be alert to the possibilities of drug use and child abuse.

Our world is changing, but children aren't. They are as impressionable and trusting as ever, and they deserve our attention, even when it is limited by necessity in terms of time.

Listening to Children

In a society where time for communication is precious and opportunities for intimacy rare, we get out of the habit of careful listening and observing. The moments a child of mine once called "a piece of quiet" are few and far between, as parents dash to and from the microwave oven after an exhausting day's work. Television and videos bombard us with so-called "relaxation," and it's easy to forget about the stimulus a child may be receiving from the violent images of a newscast or a furtive glimpse of some sexually explicit drama.

Teachers too have tremendous time pressures as well as the charge of educating and caring about not just a group of youngsters but each individual child within the group. This is a task long undervalued and under-rewarded, but it is crucial to bringing up alert, confident, well-educated children. If we think about how hard it is to notice and digest changes in one child's behavior, the idea of trying to do the same with 25 or 30 children at once is awesome.

Sometimes behavior, not words, will be the child's way of "talking," the adult's clue to an unspoken but troubling concern. Using eyes and ears, teachers and parents can listen and answer, then communicate with each other to formulate strategies for helping the children in their care.

Using Books to Respond

As children begin to ask questions and make comments about big issues that confuse and worry them, parents and teachers must respond. Responses need to be just that—responses, not lectures. (An answer, after all, usually leads to another question.) Information must be accurate and age appropriate.

Young children should not be overwhelmed with facts more complex than they are mature enough to process, and this is one important reason why providing unsolicited information or sharing a book above the child's level of comprehension can be confusing rather than helpful.

Life allows ample exposure to many of the tough topics covered in this book. Let's take *birth*, the usual beginning of our discussions of *sex* with children, as an example.

Three-year-old Esther refused to paint, touch play dough, or go near anything gooey at school. Her teacher noticed that she *would* play at the water table, and she spent a lot of time washing her hands. Other than that, her play was constricted and listless. Mom was pregnant and due in about two months. Esther's behavior continued in a fashion different from her usual enthusiastic style until after the birth of her sibling. As soon as Mom came home from the hospital, Esther showed joy and relief, experimenting at school within the full range of available activities.

This is a case in which a book with simple text and photographs, such as *We Are Having a Baby*, might have brought some early relief by demystifying the impending event. It would also have reassured Esther that Mom was not going to a hospital because she was sick and that Mom would be there for just a brief period of time before returning home.

In an instance of anxiety about impending *birth*, coupled with *sibling rivalry*, four-year-old Jim is saying, "When this baby comes, we're going to dump it in the garbage can!" No actual object of rivalry is in sight, so maybe he's anxious about the birth as well. *A Baby for Max* would be one of several possible books for Jim. ("Maxine" would have just as much impact: sex likeness takes a backseat to story line, especially in early childhood.) Reading it to him without comment, the parent or teacher can observe whether or not Jim wants to have it read again, goes back independently to look at the pictures, asks some specific questions, or makes statements that indicate more precisely where his worries lie. *Nobody Asked ME If I Wanted A Baby Sister* or an additional book about the birth process may be in order.

A five-year-old is concerned with *death*. He has started asking questions and making statements that his parents find hard to address. He has not experienced a death in the immediate family or been exposed to the demise of a beloved animal. He's been picking up on conversations between adults and has had some exposure to media coverage. This is what he's been saying:

> "I don't want to be an astronaut. I don't want to die."
>
> "It's not true that just old people die. That little girl died." (Reference to a publicized abuse/murder in New York City.)
>
> "Does everything and everybody die?"

The above thoughts are big ones for a child of five, somewhat precociously conceptual. His parents are using a book called *Lifetimes* to help him accept and understand the life cycle in a way that will not frighten him.

With older children, our need to talk with them about a tough topic may arise from the "community grapevine." Instead of ignoring rumors about drug or alcohol abuse, for instance, we can use them as a way to begin a conversation with our maturing youngster.

> "Johnny, I've heard a lot of talk around town about kids on your grade level drinking. I don't know what's going on myself, but I've been reading a book called *Not My Kid*. It made me think that you might be able to help me understand what kids today really think about drinking . . . and drugs."

On a more personal level, we may observe a child's behavior change. Dana, that bubbly and effervescent girl, has started dragging around the house and classroom. She's out visiting friends much more often after school, isn't getting her homework done, is eating less, and looks strangely teary. Matt, on the other hand, who used to be so even tempered, is showing sudden mood swings: Sometimes you can't stop him from talking, and at other moments you can't get a word out of him.

The above behaviors *may* indicate perfectly normal preteen hormonal changes. Or they may not. When in doubt, it's better to pay attention to a possible warning signal. Read up on drug and alcohol abuse symptoms, sex, child abuse, and other issues that could lie at the root of the changes. Your objective is to be informed, not panicked! Make sure you feel supportive, rather than suspicious, as you open up a dialogue. Keep your goal in mind: to make sure that your child knows you're on his side and that you want to help. If you meet with a "turn-off" the first time, don't give up. You've given out the message that you care, and a slightly different opening the next time around may bring a very different response.

Think of books as "tools." Use them to help you respond to young children. With older ones, let your child see you reading a book on a tough subject, or ask her to read one (on her own age level) and let you know what she thinks. Talk to the teacher if you're the parent; talk to the parent if you're the teacher. Discuss your concerns with the school counselor and see if some intervention may be necessary. Above all, remember that you are not alone. Problems *can* be worked through and brought to successful conclusions.

3

WHEN IS
A CHILD
READY?

Knowing something about children's abilities to understand their world can be useful as we try to help them
deal with the scarier and more confusing aspects of life.

Very Young Children

Very young children, toddlers through five- or six-year-
olds, think in concrete, literal ways. They are rapidly
adding to their vocabulary, yet they often misinterpret

words. When I was five, I remember thinking that a ferryboat was a "fairy boat"—just full of fairies from the magical tales that were read to me! The word *ferry* had no meaning, and therefore, I didn't understand the concept but used my imagination instead.

When children are very small, we make sure to guard them carefully and to know where they are. We have to be equally sure not to expect too much of them or to burden them with our fears. We should try to make certain that the messages we convey are connected to immediate happenings in their lives.

Trying to shield our youngest against the dangers of an uncertain world, we tell him, "*Never* talk to, or go off with, a stranger." We try to do this in a way that won't inhibit him from smiling or making friends with new adults in the future. We also assess what the word "stranger" means to him. Perhaps we change it to "a person you don't know." What we usually forget to think about is that the warning itself would probably be unimportant if a stranger offered him ice cream! Ice cream would simply be more significant at that moment than our carefully thought-out caution. What to do? Let him know it's permissible to express his feelings if he *doesn't* like something or someone, but protect him from his own inability to make reasoned choices at this stage.

Our youngest children also indulge in a phenomenon called "magical thinking." At two, Janet thinks that there really *is* a Man in the Moon because Daddy pointed out his face. When she is five, Janet's mother and father decide to separate, and she has a reaction that is completely logical to her, if not to the adults around her. She's been particularly upset with her mother lately and has had tantrums if Daddy doesn't come home early enough to read her a bedtime story. She sort of wishes Dad took care of her all the time. The shock of being told that her father won't live at home any more is compounded by her feeling that if she'd only been *good* enough, Mom and Dad and Janet would still be together.

Here are some "rules of thumb" for adults to follow when talking with these youngest children.

- Tell them just as much as you think they want to know, based on their questions and their behavior; don't tell them everything *you* know.

- Protect them in potentially dangerous situations.

- Encourage them to be independent in situations that are manageable.

- Tell them you love them.

- Tell them they are special and wonderful, and that it's okay to make mistakes—everybody does.

- Let them know how important they are to you—and as unique individuals.

Middle Years Children

Middle years children between the ages of six or seven and the preteen years are gradually increasing their ability to "think big." It's impossible to chart a perfect developmental timetable according to age, because each child develops at his own pace. You may have noticed that children don't learn to read, or write, at the same moment in time. Over the years I've seen three-year-old readers (who were read to at home, but given no formal instruction of any kind), four-year-old writers whose invented spelling was totally understandable, and six- and seven-year-olds—no less bright, no less talented—who were slowly acquiring these abstract skills.

One of my most meaningful discoveries occurred when, as a public-school teacher, I was "promoted" from teaching first grade to a second grade classroom. Concepts I'd knocked myself out trying to teach to first graders were gobbled up overnight by second grade children! A miracle? No, indeed. They were able to play with and then retain ideas in more advanced ways. It's important to apply an understanding of intellectual development, that gradual acquisition of the ability to conceptualize in increasingly abstract ways, when discussing tough topics with middle years children. But it is still, equally, important to continue to give them the protection, love, and support that will underpin their self-esteem and make them better able to handle the unexpected.

Preteens

When we talk about preteens today, it's necessary to think "younger" than we used to. Hormonal and related emotional changes formerly associated with 12- and 13-year-olds are now reaching down to the "9 to 12" range. These youngsters are exposed to more than their parents were—in terms of stimuli from the media and from their peers at school and in the neighborhood.

Yes, drugs *are* being "dealt," no matter how much we'd like to pretend they aren't. Sexual experimentation is starting much earlier than 20 years ago, and there is now a major health threat more frightening than any venereal disease—AIDS.

A frank talk about how AIDS (acquired immunodeficiency syndrome) can be contracted is possible with preadolescents. They can understand that blood transfusions, dirty needles, and homosexual practices can transmit the disease. But it is essential in any detailed discussion of AIDS that we *reassure* our children. Going to the doctor or the hospital to have blood taken is *not* a threat, and the crush 11-year-old Sam has on 15-year-old Martin is normal, old-fashioned "hero worship."

If you've had an open, communicative relationship with your child throughout her early and middle years, you have most likely developed skills that will permit you to continue that communication now, even if it breaks down from time to time.

The preteen years are ideal for introducing novels on sensitive issues, allowing children to feel they are not isolated or unique in their feelings of insecurity and anxiety. Other people not only understand their dilemmas but also write about them!

By this point in maturation, children are able to think in ways that are large and abstract enough to allow for complex conversations with adults. This is a good time for you to read a book *with* your child. You read it, then she reads it. He reads it, then you read it. Or you preread, then read aloud. Sometimes it seems more natural for mother to talk or read with daughter, and son with father, but it may just as likely be the other way round. In some cases, family style dictates that everyone read together in a period of sharing. All of this can lead to good, meaningful conversation.

For toddlers through 12-year-olds, books can take the role of an objective, informed "other person," making it easier to connect with children on a feeling level as well as a verbal level of communication.

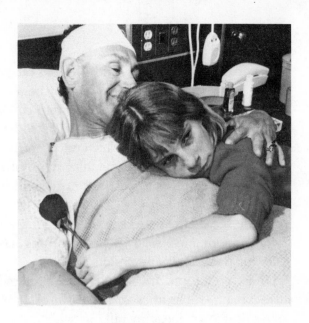

4

TOUGH TOPICS
AND
BOOK LISTS

In the suggested reading lists that follow each of the tough topics, you will find books in print to buy or order from your local bookstore or school bookfair, or to borrow from the library. They were chosen to be helpful, and they reflect my personal views and taste in children's literature.*

*Many fine illustrators have enriched the texts that follow, particularly books written specifically for young children. If names have been omitted it is simply because finding a book to fit a particular need is the purpose of the lists.

Fictional stories or informational books can be equally effective, and keep in mind that books for the very young may be surprisingly useful with more mature children as well.

Books for very young children are listed first, followed by selections for middle years and preteen youngsters, and ending with books for adults to inform and help them answer children's questions in an accurate, comfortable way.

While some books are written for children to read to themselves or have read to them, others have separate texts for both adult and child.

Under each topic the book lists are prefaced by a short introduction, sometimes in the form of an anecdote, to spark your own ideas in talking with toddlers through 12-year-olds. In each list, the titles are followed by descriptive comments.

Abuse

Although sexual abuse is horrifying, and perhaps the type most often brought to our attention, abuse is not only sexual. It also exists in the form of physical punishment, verbal sarcasm or "tongue-lashing," and simple, devastating neglect.

If you, as the adult in the situation, feel you're on the verge of losing control, there are ways to get help. "Parents Anonymous" has a national hotline number (toll free 1-800-421-0353) with local numbers available through directory assistance in most cities, and the National Child Abuse Hotline number is staffed 24 hours a day (toll free 1-800-4-A-CHILD).

Children also must know that help is available. They should be alert to potentially dangerous situations and feel comfortable in telling adults when they are worried or frightened. It is equally essential to make sure children know they are loved and respected, because we don't want them to lose a sense of openness and trust.

Establishing trust between you and your child will lay the foundation for his or her protection. And sharing a book is a tangible way to open avenues of communication.

Listed below, you will find titles of books that deal directly with abuse. Remember also that books focusing on children's abilities to express themselves, and on issues of self-esteem, can lay a secure foundation, beginning with the early years.

SUGGESTED READING: ABUSE

VERY YOUNG CHILDREN

Benjamin Rabbit and the Stranger Danger by Irene Keller. Nashville, TN: Ideals Publishing Corp., 1985. Subtitled *What a Child Needs to Know About Strangers*, this book uses animals as a vehicle to make young children aware of potentially dangerous situations. Ages 3 to 7.

Chilly Stomach by Jeannette Caines. New York: Harper & Row, 1986. Two young friends of different racial backgrounds talk about the "chilly stomach" Sandy gets when her Uncle Jim fondles her, and Jill gives Sandy the courage to tell her parents. Ages 3 to 7.

It's My Body (English) or *Mi Cuerpo Es Mio* (Spanish) by Lory Freeman. Seattle, WA: Parenting Press, Inc., 1983. A picture book available in English and Spanish to help young children learn about good and bad touching. Ages 3 to 7.

Private Zone by Frances S. Dayee. New York: Warner Books, 1988. This "read together" book for parents and children helps little ones identify private areas of their bodies. Includes advice for adults. Ages 3 to 7.

Something Happened and I'm Scared to Tell You by Patricia Kehoe. Seattle, WA: Parenting Press, Inc., 1987. This book is subtitled *A Book for Young Children, Victims of Abuse*. An imaginary lion gets his young friend to talk about the scary things that happened and manages to give a nonthreatening but accurate lesson about sexual abuse in the process. Ages 3 to 7.

Strangers by Dorothy Chlad. Chicago: Children's Press, 1982. Little Susie tells other children about strangers and how to be careful around people you don't know. There are some good safety rules here, but adults may want to soften the negative tone a little. Ages 3 to 7.

Middle Years Children

Close to Home by Oralee Wachter. New York: Scholastic, Inc., 1986. Four stories explore feelings about what's safe and what's not. This book is written for children to read to themselves, but an adult's preread would lay the groundwork for good talk. Ages 7 to 9.

Don't Hurt Me, Mama by Muriel Stanek. Niles, IL: Albert Whitman & Co., 1983. A simple story that tells a lot about the complex feelings of frustration, love, and anger compounded in a child abuse situation. Told from the child's point of view. Ages 5 to 7.

It's O.K. to Say No! by Robin Lenett with Bob Crane. New York: Tor Books, 1985. Subtitled *A Parent/Child Manual for the Protection of Children*, this book contains five short chapters for parents followed by stories for children. It deals with the sensitive subject of saying "no" to uncomfortable situations involving body safety. Ages 7 to 9.

My Body Is Private by **Linda Walvoord Girard. Niles, IL: Albert Whitman & Co., 1984.** Julie's warm relationship with Mom allows her to talk about the uncomfortable feelings she has toward Uncle Ted. To her surprise, saying "no" to her uncle results in a better relationship for both. Ages 5 to 7.

No More Secrets for Me by **Oralee Wachter. Boston: Little, Brown & Co., 1984.** While Wachter's *Close to Home* is concerned with abduction, this book has a group of stories for youngsters about sexual abuse situations. Ages 7 to 9.

PRETEENS

Don't Hurt Laurie! by **Willo Davis Roberts. New York: Aladdin Books, 1988.** Laurie calls her mother "Annabelle" because she doesn't want to think of her as "Mother" anymore. This novel tells the moving and terrible story of a young girl's physical abuse by a parent, her many trips to the hospital, and her courage as she sets out to save herself.

Feeling SAFE Feeling STRONG by **Janice E. Rench and Susan Neiburg Terkel. Minneapolis, MN: Lerner Publications, 1984.** The aim of this book is to help young people understand the differences between healthy touching and sexual abuse. Subtitled *How to Avoid Sexual Abuse and What to Do If It Happens to You*, it provides stories followed by facts that all children of this age should know. Ages 9 to 12.

MAC by **John MacLean. Boston: Houghton Mifflin Co., 1987.** A powerful novel that probes the emotions of a young teenage boy, just discovering interest in the opposite sex, who is molested during a routine physical examination by a male doctor. This book could be used to address a specific situation, or to alert parents to the intense feelings of guilt and shame assumed by innocent youngsters if they are abused.

ADULTS

By Silence Betrayed: Sexual Abuse of Children in America by **John Crewdson. Boston: Little, Brown & Co., 1988.** This comprehensive study, written by a Pulitzer Prize-winning journalist, is up-to-date, down-to-earth, and includes chapters on therapy and prevention.

The Silent Children: A Parent's Guide to the Prevention of Child Sexual Abuse by **Linda T. Sanford. New York: McGraw-Hill, Inc., 1982.** Helps parents identify ways to enable children to be assertive and self-confident. Addresses self-esteem and speaks to families of all backgrounds.

Your Child's Self-Esteem by **Dorothy C. Briggs. New York: Doubleday & Co., 1975.** A clear, helpful, practical text, still in print after many years, that provides suggestions about how to enhance children's self-worth.

Adoption

Often, families adopting an infant make the conscious decision to use the word *adoption* from the very beginning: "You're my wonderful little adopted boy!"

At a later stage their youngster asks, "Why is that lady so fat?" Answering, "She's going to have a baby, Joey, just the way your biological mother did. But we *asked* for *you* to be our little boy," the parents go on to provide accurate but simple information that Joey can digest. The word *adoption* is introduced into his vocabulary, and a special feeling is transmitted by his hearing "We loved you from the very first moment we saw you!"

More and more families are deciding to adopt older children, some from foreign countries, and there are many varieties of adoptive families. Foster parents may become so attached to a child in their care that they will petition to adopt. There is also an increase in the number of adoptions by single parents.

Children will, of course, have individual questions in different situations and at different ages. Here are some helpful books that make the concept of adoption more understandable and reinforce a natural, warm tone in parent/child discussions.

SUGGESTED READING: ADOPTION

VERY YOUNG CHILDREN

Abby by Jeannette Caines. New York: Harper Juvenile, 1984. As we get to know this close black family, we find out from Kevin how it feels to be the older child when a little sister is adopted. Ages 3 to 7.

The Adopted One by Sara B. Stein. New York: Walker & Co., 1979. Part of the Open Family Series with large photographs and texts for both children and adults, this book is straightforward and reassuring at the same time. Ages 3 to 5.

The Chosen Baby, 3rd ed., by Valentina P. Wasson. New York: Harper Juvenile, 1977. A classic since 1939, this updated edition has new illustrations. Ages 3 to 7.

I Am Adopted by Susan Lapsley. Topsfield, MA: Salem House, 1974. Sophie and Charles are two adopted toddlers in a happy family where adoption is already an accepted subject. Ages toddler to 3.

Katie-Bo: An Adoption Story by Iris L. Fisher. New York: Adama Books, 1988. Jim and his brother Ted are expecting a new baby—but this time Mom and Dad are adopting a little girl from Korea! The tone of this story rings true as Jim tells about the social worker's role, feelings of anxiety and anticipation, the joyful arrival, and Katie-Bo's acceptance into the family. Ages 3 to 7.

A Look at Adoption by Margaret S. Pursell. Minneapolis, MN: Lerner Publications, 1977. This photographic essay takes a look at adoption from its very beginnings, showing children and parents of different backgrounds. Photographs can be discussed with youngest children; text can be read to older ones. Ages 3 to 7.

MIDDLE YEARS CHILDREN AND PRETEENS

Being Adopted by Maxine B. Rosenberg. New York: Lothrop, Lee & Shepard Books, 1984. Photographs and story of a family whose children have different racial roots. Ages 7 to 12.

How It Feels to Be Adopted by Jill Krementz. New York: Alfred A. Knopf, 1988. Children of differing ages share their personal feelings about adoption. For adults and children to read together. Ages 7 to 12.

"Why Was I Adopted?" by Carole Livingston. Secaucus, NJ: Lyle Stuart, Inc., 1986. The somewhat "savvy" tone of this book places it for middle years and older children. Cartoonlike illustrations accompany straightforward information plus a good question and answer section. Ages 7 to 12.

ADULTS

Adoption: Parenthood Without Pregnancy by Charlene
    Canape. New York: Avon Books, 1988. Written by an
    adoptive parent, the author tells about the emotional
    strains of infertility and includes chapters on foreign
    adoption, special needs children, and single-parent
    adoption. The generous appendices include informa-
    tion on support groups.

Successful Adoption, rev. ed., by Jacquelin Horner Plumez.
    New York: Harmony Books, 1987. A clearly pre-
    sented and comprehensive guide to the adoption pro-
    cess, this book includes sections on telling children
    about adoption and searching for origins.

Birth

Pregnancy and birth are usually the first subjects we
discuss with our children within the larger theme of sex.
Children, like Bonnie in the story below, are often anxious before the birth of a sibling. Will Mom be okay?
What will happen afterwards?

> Bonnie Brown's mother is expecting a baby in a few
> months. Although friends have given ongoing advice
> about what to say and when to say it, Mrs. Brown has not
> felt confident about discussing the impending birth with
> Bonnie.
> Now that she's "showing," however, Mrs. Brown has
> noticed a change in her daughter's behavior. Come to
> think of it, Bonnie also seemed anxious during those
> weeks of morning sickness!

At a local bookstore, Mrs. Brown asks for help in selecting books. She wants appropriate suggestions for facing her dilemma and other books to read to Bonnie directly. Later, she shares one of the books with Mr. Brown, and together they decide on a children's book to begin a talk about pregnancy and birth with their little girl.

Knowing that Bonnie will be ready to hear only so much and that he'll need to be sensitive to her responses, Mr. Brown can confidently say, "Here's one called *We Are Having a Baby*. Let's start with that."

SUGGESTED READING: BIRTH

VERY YOUNG CHILDREN

A Baby for Max by Kathryn Lasky. New York: Aladdin Books, 1987. Photographs help us feel Max's anxiety and pleasure during his mother's pregnancy and the birth of his baby sister. Ages 3 to 5.

Before You Were Born by Margaret Sheffield. New York: Alfred A. Knopf, 1984. A beautiful book to help you explain pregnancy and birth to a curious young child. Graphic but always tasteful. Ages 3 to 7.

Everett Anderson's Nine Months' Long by Lucille Clifton. New York: Henry Holt & Co., 1987. This book tells how endless mother's pregnancy may seem to a child anticipating his sibling's birth. Short chapters of verse evoke the mood of waiting for Everett Anderson's sister to arrive. Ages 3 to 5.

The Family: PARENTS by J. M. Parramón and Carme Solé Vendrell. Hauppage, NY: Barron's Educational Series, 1987. Simple, colorful illustrations and a spare text give young children an idea of what birth means from the parents' point of view. Available in Spanish as well as English, this book concludes with pages for parents and teachers. Ages toddler to 5.

How You Were Born by Joanna Cole. New York: William Morrow & Co., 1985. Good for thinking about birth from the young child's perspective, this book includes advice for parents and was designed for a shared experience. Ages 3 to 7.

New Baby by Emily Arnold McCully. New York: Harper Juvenile, 1988. A new baby is born to the "Mouse Family"! This is a wordless book whose evocative pictures will provide their own text as adult and child turn pages together. Ages toddler to 3.

The New Baby by Fred Rogers. New York: G. P. Putnam Sons, 1985. A Mr. Rogers "First Experience" book with clear text and large color photographs. Ages toddler to 5.

See How You Grow by Dr. Patricia Pearse and Edwina Riddell. Hauppage, NY: Barron's Educational Series, 1988. This "lift-the-flap" body book is tasteful and also chock-full of information about the birth process, which is examined within the larger concept of growth. Ages 3 to 7.

So That's How I Was Born! by Dr. Robert Brooks. New York: Little Simon/Simon & Schuster, 1983. A young friend upsets Joey with her story of how babies are born. A sensitive and responsive mom and dad give him time to formulate his own questions and provide accurate, simple answers. Ages 3 to 7.

That New Baby by Sara B. Stein. New York: Walker & Co., 1984. A helpful and psychologically sound preparation for birth in the family. Written for adults and children to share together, with separate texts for both. Ages 3 to 5.

Waiting for Jennifer by Kathryn O. Galbraith. New York: Margaret K. McElderry Books, 1987. Nan and Thea wait patiently for Mama's baby to arrive. What a surprise when "Jennifer" turns out to be "?". Ages 3 to 7.

We Are Having a Baby by Vicki Holland. New York: Charles Scribner's Sons, 1972. A little girl's experiences around the birth of a new baby, enhanced by photographs. Ages toddler to 3.

You Were Born on Your Very First Birthday by Linda W. Girard. Niles, IL: Albert Whitman & Co., 1983. Gentle illustrations help describe the birth process in a story for the young child. Ages 3 to 5.

MIDDLE YEARS CHILDREN AND PRETEENS

See the Suggested Reading: Sex, and consider some of the books for younger children.

ADULTS

Make Room for Twins by Terry P. Alexander. New York: Bantam Books, 1987. Multiple births are much more common today than previously. This comprehensive guide to pregnancy and delivery of twins can help reduce anxiety at the prospect of more than one baby.

Sharing Birth by Carl Jones. New York: Quill, 1985. Written by a father for other fathers who want to give support to their wives during labor, this book also contains a section for families who wish children to be present at the birth of a sibling.

Death

How can we help children express and handle feelings about the finality of death? This is a particularly difficult question to answer if we ourselves are feeling distraught. Hard though it seems, the best way to go about it is to face the fact that children need to know the truth.

> Bob Green's mother, a former dog trainer, is beside herself with grief over the death of the family's Irish setter. Mrs. Green is torn about how to tell Bob that Fido has not returned from the veterinarian's office. She is consumed with decisions concerning burial or cremation, and whether or not there should be a funeral.
>
> Bob thinks his mother seems distant and preoccupied. He wonders if he's done something wrong.
>
> Mr. Green remembers seeing a book about the life cycle—not a book about dogs, but about birth and death. He stops by the local bookstore on his way home from work.
>
> That evening—one short book, many tears, and much relief later—the family has decided on plans for Fido's funeral. They may get another dog in the future, but not right now. Privately, Mrs. Green tells her husband about Aunt Sally's terminal illness. Perhaps today's experience will pave the way for their child to cope with the death of a beloved family member.

If death can be accepted as part of the life cycle (see *Lifetimes* and *Yonder* below) and faced sadly but squarely as in the vignette above, the painful deaths of people we love can fall within a context that promises eventual recovery.

SUGGESTED READING: DEATH

VERY YOUNG CHILDREN

About Dying by Sara B. Stein. New York: Walker & Co., 1984. Little Eric learns about death. Story with photographs and separate texts for little ones and parents. One of a fine series about tough topics. Ages 3 to 5.

Annie and the Old One by Miska Miles. New York: Atlantic-Little, Brown & Co., 1971. The story of a young Navaho girl's relationship to her grandmother. Grandmother is wise and knows that, when the rug is woven, she will die. How Annie continues to help her weave forms the climax of this moving story. Ages 3 to 7.

The Dead Bird by Margaret Wise Brown. New York: Harper Juvenile, 1958; Dell, 1979. This book was one of the earliest written about death for young children. In a sensitive story of the discovery of a dead bird, children grieve, plan a funeral, and movingly return to their everyday activities. Ages 3 to 7.

Goodbye, Max by Holly Keller. New York: Greenwillow Books, 1987. Young Ben is angry about the death of Max, the family dog, even though he was old. To make things worse, Max died while Ben was at school. Solace eventually comes in the form of a new puppy. Ages 3 to 7.

Grandpa's Slide Show by Debora Gould. New York: Lothrop, Lee & Shepard Books, 1987. Watching slide shows with Grandpa is a family pleasure. When Grandpa dies, Sam and Douglas share the feelings and events with their mother and grandmother, and experience memories of Grandpa in a family "show" without him. Ages 3 to 7.

I Had a Friend Named Peter by Janice Cohn. New York: William Morrow & Co., 1987. This gentle book can help adults talk to children about the death of a friend. Ages 3 to 5.

I'll Always Love You by Hans Wilhelm. New York: Crown Publishers, 1985. Few words and tender illustrations make this an appropriate story for little ones encountering death for the first time. A beloved dog, Elfie, dies. Ages toddler to 5.

Last Week My Brother Anthony Died by Martha Whitmore Hickman. Nashville, TN: Abingdon Press, 1984. The subject of this book is the death of a newborn sibling. Helpful reading for families encountering this specific tragedy. Ages 3 to 7.

Lifetimes: The Beautiful Way to Explain Death to Children by Bryan Mellonie and Robert Ingpen. New York: Bantam Books, 1983. Death is explained as part of the life cycle. A valuable reading experience at any age. Ages 3 and up.

Nana Upstairs & Nana Downstairs by Tomie de Paola. New York: Puffin Books, 1978; Putnam, 1987. Tommy's grandmother and great-grandmother are both part of his extended family. He loves them and grieves when they die, but growing up helps put loss in perspective. Ages 3 to 7.

The Saddest Time by Norma Simon. Niles, IL: Albert Whitman & Co., 1986. Poems and stories explore the deaths of a range of significant people in the lives of children. Ages 3 to 7.

Saying Goodbye to Grandma by Marcia Sewall. Boston: Clarion Books, 1988. Although this story concerns the death of seven-year-old Suzie's Grandma, it could be used with young *and* middle years children. Sensitive illustrations alone might lead the younger child through the rituals of a funeral (which include a "viewing"). For all, a feeling of family solidarity and the enduring resilience of childhood are communicated.

The Tenth Good Thing About Barney by Judith Viorst. New York: Aladdin Books, 1988. It's a sad time when a little boy's cat, Barney, dies. At the burial, only nine "good things" come to mind, but time brings an important tenth. Ages 3 to 7.

The Two of Them by Aliki. New York: Mulberry Books, 1987. This is a simple history of the relationship between a little girl and her grandfather. She is not ready to have him die but remembering helps. An honest yet tender story. Ages 3 to 7.

When Violet Died by Mildred Kantrowitz. New York: Parents' Magazine Press, 1973. Amy and Eva know that their bird, Violet, is going to die. Their friends help with the burial and funeral. Just as it seems that "nothing will last forever," the thought that their cat will soon have kittens makes the girls feel better. Ages 3 to 7.

Yonder by Tony Johnston. New York: Dial Books, 1988. A graceful and poetic book about the passage of time. Illustrations by Lloyd Bloom play a large part in describing the history of a family. Ages 3 to 7.

MIDDLE YEARS CHILDREN AND PRETEENS

Bridge to Terabithia by Katherine Patterson. New York: Crowell Junior Books, 1977; Trophy, 1987; Scholastic, 1988. A moving novel that explores feelings aroused by the loss of a close friend. Ages 9 to 12.

Charlotte's Web by E. B. White. New York: Harper Juvenile, 1952. This classic story hardly needs introducing. Charlotte, the gray barnyard spider, plays a central role, and the way she faces her death is both inevitable and healing. Ages 7 to 12.

Face at the Edge of the World by Eve Bunting. Boston: Clarion Books, 1987. A novel for mature preteens and teenagers which examines a teen suicide from the standpoint of a friend's close look at young Charlie Curtis' final weeks of life.

How It Feels When a Parent Dies by Jill Krementz. New York: Alfred A. Knopf, 1988. The stories of 18 children who lost one of their parents are told in their own words and illustrated with photographs. Helpful for adults as well as children. Ages 7 to 12.

To Hell with Dying by Alice Walker. New York: Harcourt Brace Jovanovich, 1988. Mr. Sweet's impact on Pulitzer prize-winning author Walker's childhood is recounted here for children as she contemplates his death. Catherine Deeter's illustrations add to the portrait of an unusual and charismatic black guitar player.

ADULTS

See Suggested Reading: Separation.

Differences

Black . . . white . . . tall . . . tiny . . . dark . . . fair . . . slim . . . heavy . . . male . . . female . . . fast . . . slow—children notice differences. Children often talk about differences without inhibition.

My friend, born with part of an arm missing, does not disguise it. The kindergarten class he is visiting has mixed reactions. Some children stare, eyes wide, faces blank. Others come directly up to him. A boy asks, "Why is your arm like that?" My friend says, "I was born that way," and he continues during his visit to use the stump of his arm efficiently and unaffectedly, as if it were complete with hand and fingers.

A young black mother tells me that her five-year-old daughter is asking "Why is my hand a different color from his hand? Why are our faces a different color?" It won't take care of all of the questions sure to follow if mother answers, "There's a substance in the skin called 'pigment' that makes some skin light, some skin dark." But it's an opening into a discussion about the differences among us all—and the likenesses. We are all human, and therefore alike in many ways. We are all unique, and therefore different from one another. Some of us are similar through racial or national background, and we may identify strongly with that background. There are endless variations to the theme.

Informing children about all kinds of differences, making children comfortable with their own special characteristics—whatever they may be—is our task as parents and teachers. Although we cannot solve the problems of the world, we can be direct and helpful, accepting and reinforcing.

Books in the following list reflect my personal view of the many ways "differences" can be understood and my belief that adults can begin to establish this concept with very young children.

SUGGESTED READING: DIFFERENCES

VERY YOUNG CHILDREN

Big and Little by The Philip Lief Group, Inc. New York: Random House, 1988. A cardboard "Matchem" book, color coded, to help very small children think about the concept of opposites. Ages toddler to 3.

The Boy Who Didn't Believe in Spring by Lucille Clifton. New York: E. P. Dutton, 1988. Two young friends from different ethnic backgrounds, King Shabazz and Tony Polito, set out to see for themselves if spring is really coming. Ages 3 to 7.

The Cross-Eyed Rabbit by Claude Boujon. New York: Margaret K. McElderry Books, 1988. How one of three rabbit brothers, different from the others, saves his siblings from a hungry fox. Ages 3 to 5.

Crow Boy by Taro Yashima. New York: Viking Press, 1955; Puffin Books, 1976. In print for over 30 years, the story of Chibi, a strange little Japanese boy left alone by all his classmates, is as fresh and telling today as when it was written. Find out how Chibi's unique gifts triumph as he becomes "Crow Boy." Ages 3 to 7.

The Family: Children by J. M. Parramón and María Ruis. Hauppage, NY: Barron's Educational Series, 1987. A book for the very young to help them think about how all children are the same as they move through the growth process, even though all children are different. Also available in Spanish as *Los Niños*. Ages toddler to 3.

Here Are My Hands by Bill Martin, Jr., and John Archambault. New York: Henry Holt & Co., 1987. All kinds of kids doing all kinds of things, shown with a rhyming text, invite the very young to act out what they see and hear along with the children in the illustrations. Ages toddler to 3.

Leo the Late Bloomer, reissue ed., by Robert Kraus. New York: Windmill Books, 1987. Leo, a young tiger, can't seem to do "anything" as his worried parents observe. "Late blooming" children—and their parents—will feel a lot better after being reassured by this book. Ages 3 to 7.

Opposites by Rosalinda Knightley and Sara Lynne. Boston: Little, Brown & Co., 1986. Big words and simple, colorful pictures show the meaning of opposites. Ages toddler to 3.

The Tamarindo Puppy and Other Poems by Charlotte Pomerantz. New York: Greenwillow Books, 1980. A unique mixing of Spanish and English in delightful poems for young children that can be understood by those who speak either language—or both. Ages 3 to 7.

Toby in the Country, Toby in the City by Maxine Zohn Bozzo. New York: Greenwillow Books, 1982. Two boys have the same name, but live in very different environments. Ages 3 to 5.

Who Am I? by Barry Head and Jim Sequin. Northbrook, IL: Hubbard Scientific, 1975. We see a little hearing-impaired girl with her black family and friends asking persistently "Who am I?" until she finds the answer: "ME!" Photographs of many differing moods to provoke discussion. Ages 3 to 5.

MIDDLE YEARS CHILDREN AND PRETEENS

The Boy from Over There by Tamar Bergman. Boston: Houghton Mifflin Co., 1988. Avramik, a young refugee child from Eastern Europe who joins a kibbutz in Israel immediately after the end of World War II, seems strange and silent to the other children. His eventual acceptance is part of this rich and haunting story. Ages 9 to 12.

The Friendship by Mildred Taylor. New York: Dial Books, 1987. Set in 1933, this is the true story of a white man and black man's friendship at a time and in a place where such a human alliance was fraught with danger. Ages 9 to 12.

The Gift-Giver by **Joyce Hansen. Boston: Clarion Books, 1989.** Replete with dialogue that illustrates and honors dialect, this novel for youngsters in the middle and upper elementary grades tells not only about a special friendship, but about life in a tough section of the Bronx. Ages 9 to 12.

A Look at Prejudice and Understanding by **Rebecca Anders. Minneapolis, MN: Lerner Publications, 1976.** Although the text is short and simple, the concept of prejudice is not a simple one to explain: In the words of a famous song, children have to be "carefully taught." Bill Cosby's words, "If you like yourself, you will work hard to judge each individual fairly," set the stage for the photographs that follow. Ages 7 to 12.

Making a New Home in America by **Maxine B. Rosenberg. New York: Lothrop, Lee & Shepard Books, 1987.** Vivid photographs enhance this book about immigrant families and their children's adjustment to life in the United States. Ages 7 to 12.

Nobody's Family Is Going to Change by **Louise Fitzhugh. New York: Sunburst/Farrar, Straus & Giroux, 1986.** Willie wants to be a tap dancer, while older sister Emma wants to be a lawyer—just the reverse of what their mother and father think should be going on. A funny and human story about expectations and differences. Ages 9 to 12.

Park's Quest by **Katherine Patterson. New York: Lodestar/ E. P. Dutton, 1988.** In trying to find out about his father, who died in Vietnam, Park discovers a surprising relative. His and Thanh's complex relationship reaches resolution at the end of Park's quest for the truth. Ages 9 to 12.

ADULTS

Clara's Heart by **Joseph Olshan. New York: Ballantine Books, 1987.** A touching story of the deep, enduring relationship between a young white boy and a black Jamaican woman.

Teacher by **Sylvia Ashton-Warner. New York: Simon & Schuster, 1986.** Ashton-Warner gives a vivid description of the method she created to teach Maori children and children of British background in the same New Zealand classroom.

Two Worlds of Childhood: U.S. and U.S.S.R. by **Urie Brofenbrenner. New York: Touchstone/Simon & Schuster, 1979.** A scholarly contrast of the rearing of American and Soviet children, both at home and in school.

Divorce

It's sobering to learn that the U.S. Census Bureau estimates approximately 50 percent of children born in the United States before 1982 will live with only one parent by the time they are 18 years old. (A new and helpful pamphlet called *Children of Divorce Resource Guide: Information Sources for Children, Parents, and Teachers* is available for $4.50 from Cornell University Rural Schools Program, Department of Education, 293 Roberts Hall, Ithaca, NY 14853–5901.)

The shock of divorce hits children hard, from the first moment of realization through weeks, months, and even years to come. Michelle's initial reaction, below, is not unusual.

Michelle walks home with a springy step and the hope that this will be "spaghetti night." Banging the door behind her, she's aware of a strange silence. The other kids are sitting in the kitchen with Mom and Dad, and nobody's saying anything.

"Michelle, come in please." Her dad's voice is tight. "I've got something to tell you. . . . Mom and I are going to get a divorce." Michelle's stomach cramps . . . she can't catch her breath. Then suddenly, with the first wrench of a sob, she goes racing to the refuge of her room.

Reading aloud and to themselves has helped this family before, and it's one of the resources available to them now. There is no simple answer to making Michelle and others like her feel better, to keep her from wondering if this is all her fault. But there are ways to try to talk to her, ways to help her feel she's not to blame and that she's not alone. Books are one of the avenues open to help ease her pain.

SUGGESTED READING: DIVORCE

VERY YOUNG CHILDREN

Always, Always by Crescent Dragonwagon. New York: Macmillan Publishing Co., 1984. A little girl tells her story of living with both divorced parents for part of each year. The details create a poignant atmosphere, but neither parent undermines the other as they both assure her they'll love her "always, always." Ages 3 to 7.

Dinosaurs Divorce by Laurene K. and Marc Brown. Boston: Little, Brown & Co., 1988. A book that can help children understand the hows and whys of coping with divorcing parents by removing the problems to "dinosaur land." Ages 3 to 7.

My Mother's House, My Father's House by C. H. Christiansen. New York: Atheneum, 1989. A young girl, obviously loved by both parents, describes the separate households in which she lives and looks forward to having a home of her own one day. Ages 3 to 7.

On Divorce by Sara B. Stein. New York: Walker & Co., 1984. An adult resource for handling children's questions and a book for young children broad enough in scope for use by intact families as well. Ages 3 to 5.

Sometimes a Family Has to Split Up by Jane Werner Watson, Robert E. Switzer, M.D., and J. Cotter Hirschberg, M.D. New York: Crown Publishers, 1988. This "read together" book for parents and children, created in cooperation with the Menninger Foundation, gets directly to the young child's feelings about divorce and is reassuring. Ages 3 to 5.

Two Places to Sleep by Joan Schuchman. Minneapolis, MN: Carolrhoda Books, 1979. David tells us about his mom and dad's divorce and about some of the reassuring things they tell him despite his feeling that *he's* divorced too. Ages 3 to 7.

Where's Daddy?: The Story of a Divorce by Beth Goff. Boston: Beacon Press, 1969. This twenty-year-old story is still in print and endorsed by the Child Study Association of America. It tells the story of "Janeydear's" feelings when Daddy leaves home. Ages 3 to 5.

MIDDLE YEARS CHILDREN

How It Feels When Parents Divorce by Jill Krementz. New York: Alfred A. Knopf, 1984. Sensitive photographs and real-life stories allow adults and children of differing ages to express their feelings. Ages 7 and up.

Mr. Rogers Talks with Families About Divorce by Claire O'Brian and Fred Rogers. New York: Berkley Publishing Group, 1987. Direct, open handling of a sensitive subject for children and parents to share together. Ages 7 and up.

There Was a Place and Other Poems by Myra Cohn Livingston. New York: Margaret K. McElderry Books, 1989. A rare collection of poems that express children's feelings as they cope with the pain and confusion of living in divided families. Ages 5 to 9.

When Mom and Dad Divorce by Steven L. Nickman. New York: Julian Messner/Simon & Schuster, 1986. A book of stories for children to read to themselves about different aspects of divorce, with suggestions by the author about things to do and ways to feel better. Ages 7 to 9.

PRETEENS

Dear Mr. Henshaw by Beverly Cleary. New York: Scholastic, Inc., 1988. Leigh's correspondence with Mr. Henshaw helps him and his divorced parents face some problems. Ages 9 to 12.

The Divorce Express by Paula Danziger. New York: Laurel Leaf/Dell Publishing Co., 1983. Although the heroine of this novel is a ninth grader, preteens can relate to her feelings as she shuttles on the "Divorce Express" to and from her parents' homes. Ages 9 to 12.

It's Not the End of the World by Judy Blume. New York: Laurel Leaf/Dell Publishing Co., 1982. A novel for youngsters that helps them see divorce as just what the title promises. Ages 9 to 12.

The Kids' Book About Single-Parent Families, ed. by Paul Dolmetsch and Alexa Shih. New York: Dolphin/

Doubleday & Co., 1985. This collaboration covers the immediate and long-range problems of living with divorced parents, as well as with single parents in other situations. "By Kids for Everyone." Ages 9 to 12.

What's Going to Happen to Me? by Eda LeShan. **New York: Aladdin Books, 1986.** A warm yet direct book which takes on the feelings aroused by divorce in a family. Ages 9 to 12.

ADULTS

See Suggested Reading: Separation.

Drugs

We know that drugs are frighteningly available to our children at younger and younger ages. It doesn't *seem* to make sense to bring up the subject too soon, and it's scary besides. But for little ones, the concept of "too much" is possible to understand. A diet of nothing but chocolate won't allow young bodies to grow and develop properly. Too much television has been labeled by one author as "the plug-in drug."

Later on, the idea that drugs endanger health and the enjoyment of life may come up at home, in conversation after exposure to a television show or newspaper item. At school, where peers may introduce a more glamorous image of narcotic substances, alcohol and drug awareness programs are often mandated curricula that need to be responsibly followed up and evaluated. (An adult recently told me that as a preteen she saw a school film on drug abuse. There was no opportunity to talk about it afterwards, and she was terrified for weeks that "pushers" lurked in her school's corridors.)

If, when the moment seems appropriate, adults can talk about drugs as life threatening, pathetic substitutes for enjoyment—and can do this in a nonjudgmental way—then the doors to communication stand open.

The first books listed in this section are stories for young children that can begin to get the "too much" concept across. These are followed by some explicit novels for older children, which should be read first by adults, and books containing information about AIDS because of the threat of transmission through shared use of contaminated needles. There are also books to bring knowledge and support to parents and teachers.

SUGGESTED READING: DRUGS

VERY YOUNG CHILDREN

The Berenstain Bears and Too Much Junk Food by Jan & Stan Berenstain. New York: Random House, 1985. An easy way to introduce your "cubs" to the "too much" concept.

The Berenstain Bears and Too Much TV by Jan & Stan Berenstain. New York: Random House, 1984. The cubs discover that giving up TV "cold turkey" has some advantages.

MIDDLE YEARS CHILDREN AND PRETEENS

The Boy Who Drank Too Much by Shep Greene. New York: Laurel Leaf/Dell Publishing Co., 1980. Story of a high school athlete who's out-of-school pressures cause him to drink. Appropriate for preteens. Ages 9 to 12.

It's O.K. to Say No to Drugs by Alan Gardner. New York: Tor Books, 1987. This parent/child manual leads readers through the "hows" and "whys" of what causes children to become involved with drugs. Addresses prevention and help and provides simple "What would you do?" stories. Ages 7 to 12.

Know About Drugs by Margaret O. Hyde and Bruce G. Hyde. New York: McGraw-Hill, Inc., 1979. A book that tells about drugs in a straightforward manner. Ages 9 to 12.

Understanding AIDS by Ethan A. Lerner. Minneapolis, MN: Lerner Publications, 1987. AIDS can be contracted from contaminated needles as well as through sexual transmission. This helpful, appropriate book contains a story and facts about drug abuse. Ages 7 to 12.

What's Happening to My Body? Books by Lynda Madaras. New York: Newmarket Press, 1987. Separate volumes for boys and for girls include information about AIDS and transmission of the disease through drug use (new editions only). Ages 9 to 12.

You Can Say No to a Drink or a Drug: What Every Kid Should Know by Susan Newman. New York: G. P. Putnam's Sons, 1986. This covers how kids can take charge of situations which involve alcohol and/or drugs. Ages 9 to 12.

ADULTS

Go Ask Alice by an anonymous teenager. New York: Avon/ Flair Books, 1982. A powerful and important book that will tell you all you need to know about how children can get hooked on drugs and what it feels like. This devastating story of adolescent needs and feelings takes a young girl from drugs to sex, abuse, and eventual death.

I'll Quit Tomorrow, rev. ed., by **Vernon E. Johnson. New York: Harper & Row, 1980.** If you need information about alcoholism and its treatment, this will give you basic and comprehensive understanding.

Not My Kid: A Parent's Guide to Kids and Drugs by **Miller Newton and Beth Polson. New York: Avon Books, 1985.** A perceptive book that will help parents identify a drug problem and advise them on what to do about it.

The Plug-in Drug by **Marie Winn. New York: Viking Press, 1985.** Excessive television viewing by children seen as similar to the influence of a drug.

Handicaps

When dealing with the reality of a handicap, it is especially important to keep in mind that every single human being in the world is unique, that differences exist between each and every person.

Maggie, a little girl I once taught when she was five years old, had cerebral palsy. She was able to move with difficulty, and had been subjected to—would *be* subjected to—many operations. Her parents and therapist worked intensively with her each day, putting her through necessary, exhausting, exercises. Maggie had a smile so engaging that it lit up the room. Children loved her. Teachers loved her. She was somehow able to embrace the world as she embraced the challenges of her handicap.

Some handicaps are visible and obvious. It is easy to tell that there is something unusual about the way a person with cerebral palsy moves, or to notice that an arm or leg is missing from an otherwise intact body. Other handicaps are more subtle—such as speech or hearing impairments and a wide range of learning disabilities.

Handicapped children and their parents face special problems coping with emotional as well as physical adjustment. Their stories are often moving and courageous.

Using books to help these families (and families of the nonhandicapped) talk about disabilities can make coming to terms with a painful reality easier to accomplish and comprehend.

SUGGESTED READING: HANDICAPS

VERY YOUNG CHILDREN

About Handicaps by Sara B. Stein. New York: Walker & Co., 1984. There is joy as well as reality in this book of photographs with a simple children's text and words of advice for adults. Ages 3 to 5.

Grandpa Doesn't Know It's Me by Donna Guthrie. New York: Human Sciences Press, Inc., 1986. Lizzy tells it like it is as Grandpa's behavior changes. Mom and Dad's explanation of Alzheimer's disease helps her understand, accept, and continue to love him. Ages 3 to 7.

Lisa and Her Soundless World by Edna S. Levine. New York: Human Sciences Press, Inc., 1984. The story of Lisa's life, without hearing, from infancy to age eight abounds with empathy and information. Ages 5 and up.

Now One Foot, Now the Other by Tomie De Paola. New York: G. P. Putnam's Sons, 1981. Tells how Bobby helps his grandfather to walk again after a stroke. Ages 3 to 7.

MIDDLE YEARS CHILDREN

Handtalk by Remy Charlip and Mary Beth Miller. New York: Aladdin Books, 1986. This book brings the reader into the world of sign language, with full-color photographs and instructions about signing. Ages 7 to 9.

Helen Keller by Margaret Davidson. New York: Scholastic, Inc., 1973. A children's biography of one of our most famous handicapped heroines. Ages 7 to 9.

A Look at Mental Retardation by Rebecca Anders. Minneapolis, MN: Lerner Publications, 1976. A factual photo/essay, brief in text but conceptually right for the middle years. Ages 7 to 9.

PRETEENS

Alzheimer's Disease: The Silent Epidemic by Julia Frank. Minneapolis, MN: Lerner Publications, 1985. A factual book for youngsters old enough to investigate this handicap from an intellectual standpoint by tracing the progress of elderly "Sarah's" disease. Ages 9 to 12.

Child of the Morning by Barbara Corcoran. New York: Atheneum, 1982. After persistent dizzy spells, Susan is diagnosed as an epileptic. A novel for children ages 9 to 12.

The Summer of the Swans by Betsy Byars. New York: Puffin Books, 1981. Sara's love for her mentally retarded brother, Charlie, is crystallized for her when he disappears. A Newbery award-winning novel. Ages 9 to 12.

What If You Couldn't . . . ? A Book of Special Needs by Janet Kamien. New York: Charles Scribner's Sons, 1979. This book helps normal children imagine what their world would be like if they were disabled. Ages 9 to 12.

ADULTS

After the Tears by **Robin Simons. New York: Harcourt Brace Jovanovich, 1987.** Subtitled *Parents Talk About Raising a Child with a Disability*, this is a book to bring strength and courage.

Learning Disabilities: A Family Affair by **Betty B. Osman. New York: Random House, 1979.** Helping children overcome learning differences—the hidden handicap—at home, at school, and out in the world.

The Misunderstood Child by **Larry B. Silver, M.D. New York: McGraw-Hill, Inc., 1988.** This guide for parents of learning-disabled children is particularly helpful in discussing the problems of older youngsters.

Reversals by **Eileen Simpson. New York: Washington Square Press, 1981.** This personal account of the author's triumph over dyslexia is a "must" for learning firsthand about children's feelings.

Illness and Health Care

In recent years, many books have been published relating to nearly every aspect of health care, and fine children's books range from works of fiction to photo-illustrated volumes. They can help to prepare children in situations like these:

Little Nick has two bedtime stories tonight. One is a comforting and familiar tale about saying "goodnight" to the moon, the other a picture book portraying a doctor's instruments in large and colorful pictures. Tomorrow Nick will be getting his six-month physical checkup.

Nancy is going to another kind of doctor's office this afternoon. Her mother borrows a book of photographs about a little girl's first trip to the dentist from Nancy's early childhood center. They'll look at it together after school.

Gabrielle's dad turns the pages of a new book as father and daughter sit side by side after breakfast on Saturday morning. "This girl's name is Anna. . . . She's really upset. Her mother's still in the hospital too, just like Mommy."

The following lists contain reassuring picture books, stories, and information about specific illnesses. *Note*: A National PTA brochure, "How to Talk to Your Child About AIDS" (available from The National PTA, 700 North Rush Street, Chicago, IL 60611-2571) may be helpful to both teachers and parents in thinking of ways to answer children's questions about today's most talked about health issue.

SUGGESTED READING: ILLNESS AND HEALTH CARE

VERY YOUNG CHILDREN

Arthur's Eyes by Marc Brown. Boston: Little, Brown & Co., 1986. Arthur and his pal learn all about vision. Ages 3 to 7.

The Berenstain Bears Visit the Dentist by Jan and Stan Berenstain. New York: Random House, 1987. Going to the dentist can be scary, but Dr. Bearson makes it fun to have clean teeth. Ages 3 to 5.

Curious George Goes to the Hospital by H. A. and Margaret Rey. Boston: Houghton Mifflin Co., 1966. The beloved monkey's adventures, this time at the hospital. Ages 3 to 7.

A Doctor's Tools by Kenny DeSantis. New York: Dodd, Mead & Co., 1985. Photographs of a doctor's tools and the accurate words that describe them, as well as doctors using their instruments. Ages 3 to 7.

Going to the Doctor by Fred Rogers. New York: G. P. Putnam's Sons, 1986. Fine preparation using vivid color photographs for a visit to the pediatrician. (Also recommended: *Going to the Dentist*.) Ages toddler to 5.

The Hospital Scares Me by Paula Z. Hogan and Kirk Hogan, M.D. Milwaukee, WI: Raintree Children's Books, 1980. With an introduction for parents and teachers, this is fine for preparation for demystifying a visit to the hospital. Ages 3 to 7.

A Hospital Story by Sara B. Stein. New York: Walker & Co., 1984. A guide for adults as well as children facing a hospital stay, with separate texts for both. Ages toddler to 5.

I Want Mama by Marjorie Weinman Sharmat. New York: Harper & Row, 1974. A little girl's mother has to go to the hospital. Coping with the experience is hard, but Daddy helps—and Mama does come home! Ages 3 to 7.

It Hurts! by Anne Sibley O'Brien. New York: Henry Holt & Co., 1986. In this sturdy board book for little ones, we see Tiffany fall down and hurt her knee, cry as her mother prepares to clean it, and emerge bandaged and smiling. Ages toddler to 3.

Little Rabbit Goes to the Doctor by J. P. Miller. New York: Random House, 1987. There are some realistic touches in this story of Little Rabbit and his mother's visit to "Dr. O'Hare." Ages toddler to 3.

My Doctor by Harlow Rockwell. New York: Harper Juvenile, 1985. Large, accurate drawings and simple story tell about a boy's trip for a checkup with his female pediatrician. Ages toddler to 5.

My Friend the Doctor by Robert E. Switzer, M.D., and Jane Werner Watson. New York: Crown Publishers, 1987. This Menninger Foundation "Read Together Book for Parents and Children" covers several different situations and many feelings related to a trip to the doctor. Ages 3 to 5.

Taryn Goes to the Dentist by Jill Krementz. New York: Crown Publishers, 1986. A sturdy board book about Taryn's first visit to her dentist, Dr. Levine. Ages toddler to 3.

A Trip to the Doctor by Margot Linn. New York: Harper Juvenile, 1988. In guessing-game format, children will enjoy uncovering the flaps of this book to find answers to questions about what will happen in the doctor's office. Ages toddler to 5.

MIDDLE YEARS CHILDREN

First Aid for Kids by Gary Fleisher, M.D. Hauppage, NY: Barron's Educational Series, 1987. A handy and durable book, this is an invaluable reference for both children and adults. Thumb tabs and space for emergency numbers are included. Can be used by all children of reading age.

My Book for Kids with Cansur by Jason Gaes. Aberdeen, SD: Melius & Peterson Publishing, 1988. Jason's autobiography of hope is written by a child for other children. It includes his own handwriting, spelling, and illustrations by his brothers. Ages 5 to 9.

No Measles, No Mumps for Me by Paul Showers. New York: Crowell Junior Books, 1980. A "Let's-Read-and-Find-Out Science Book" about health and disease. Ages 7 to 9.

Some Busy Hospital! by Seymour Reit. New York: Western Publishing Co., A Golden Book, 1985. Lots of detail and plenty of information for curious kids abound. Ages 7 to 9.

PRETEENS

Alzheimer's Disease by Elaine Landau. New York: Franklin Watts, 1987. An excellent, thorough explanation of Alzheimer's Disease, which can help preteens and adults alike to understand and join together in the care of a loved one suffering from this ailment.

Eating Disorders by Ellen Erlanger. Minneapolis, MN: Lerner Publications, 1987. An important question-and-answer book about anorexia nervosa and bulimia that examines the psychological as well as the physical symptoms and serious outcomes of these diseases. Ages 9 to 12.

It Can't Hurt Forever by Marilyn Singer. New York: Harper & Row, 1978. This is the story of a young girl whose heart problems require an operation. Ages 9 to 12.

ADULTS

Read the above books that seem appropriate to your specific situation, and learn firsthand—before your child does—about the details of any medical situation he or she will be facing.

Separation

We often think of death as the final "separation," but in fact we are dealing with separation from the moment of birth. Life quickly brings experiences of being left—with baby-sitters, in day-care centers, at school. We move from one home to another, visit grandparents for brief periods, wave good-bye to cherished loved ones.

> In an early childhood center, a little boy is weeping uncontrollably. His parents have done their best to say a cheerful good-bye, tell their child that teachers will take good care of him, and assure him that Mommy will pick him up after work—in time for supper. Ms. Park, a teacher of many years' experience, goes to a special shelf of school library books. Settling down comfortably next to Jeff, she doesn't speak but turns the pages slowly, holding the book at an angle so he can see the pictures.
> "Shawn always wanted to go to school," reads Ms. Park. "How sad Shawn looks in the next picture, just like you, Jeff. . . ." Sharing this book with his teacher is Jeff's first step towards trusting her and feeling comfortable away from home.

Because it helps to understand what a big issue separation can be, and how it affects many areas of our lives, there are several books on the following list that can help you explore your own feelings as you try to help children with theirs.

SUGGESTED READING: SEPARATION

VERY YOUNG CHILDREN

First Day of School by Helen Oxenbury. New York: Dial Books, 1983. It's hard to let Mommy leave on the first day of school, even if the teacher lets her stay awhile. A simple story to help little ones understand that teachers can take care of you and parents return to pick you up. Ages toddler to 5.

Going to Day Care by Fred Rogers. New York: G. P. Putnam's Sons, 1985. Another colorful Mr. Rogers "First Experiences" book. Vivid photographs show the beginning and end of the day, at home. In between, we see details of a day-care setting and various activities, but never at the expense of the child's feelings. Ages toddler to 5.

The Good-Bye Book by Judith Viorst. New York: Atheneum, 1988. Mom and Dad want to go out for dinner, but their son gives them a hard time until a teenage boy arrives as baby-sitter. A humorous book that can be read to slightly older, "manipulative" youngsters who still don't like the idea of saying good-bye. Ages 3 to 7.

Grandma Is Somebody Special by Susan Goldman. Niles, IL: Albert Whitman & Co., 1976. Spending the night alone at Grandma's brings its own special times and treats to a fortunate little girl. Ages 3 to 7.

Maggie Doesn't Want to Move by Elizabeth Lee O'Donnell. New York: Four Winds Press, 1987. Older brother Simon works out his own feelings about moving to a new neighborhood by telling everyone that his little sister Maggie doesn't want to move. Ages 3 to 7.

My Mom Travels a Lot by Caroline F. Bauer. New York: Puffin Books, 1985. There are good and bad things about Mom taking a trip, but she always comes home in the end. Ages 3 to 5.

The Runaway Bunny by Margaret Wise Brown. New York: Harper & Row, 1977. This classic continues to reassure little ones that even if they "run away," Mother will always find them. Ages toddler to 3.

Shawn Goes to School by Petronella Breinburg. New York: Crowell Junior Books, 1974. Shawn wants to go to school, but he has a difficult time staying at first. Ages toddler to 3.

Sometimes a Family Has to Move by Jane Werner Watson, Robert E. Switzer, M.D., and J. Cotter Hirschberg, M.D. New York: Crown Publishers, 1988. Another fine "Read Together Book for Parents & Children" by a team of experts. Ages 3 to 5.

When I Go Visiting by Anne and Harlow Rockwell. New York: Macmillan Publishing Co., 1984. A little boy spends the night at Grandma and Grandpa's. Ages 3 to 5.

MIDDLE YEARS CHILDREN

Ira Says Goodbye by Bernard Waber. Boston: Houghton Mifflin Co., 1988. A wonderfully "true to life" story of the downs and ups of having to say good-bye to your best friend. From Ira's tormenting sister to Reggie's irritating denial that moving could be anything but "Great, great, great!," this story rings true. Ages 7 to 9.

Left Behind by Carol Carrick. Boston: Clarion Books, 1989. On a class trip, Christopher is temporarily lost on the subway when he gets separated from his partner. A scary experience with a happy ending. Ages 5 to 7.

A Smooth Move by Berniece Rabe. Niles, IL: Albert Whitman & Co., 1987. Gus records all the events of his family's move across the United States from Oregon to Washington, D.C., in his private journal—a detailed and delightful account. Ages 7 to 9.

The Summer Cat by Howard Knotts. New York: Harper & Row, 1981. Leaving their "summer cat," Apple Blossom, is almost too much for Ben and Annie to bear. Ages 5 to 9.

PRETEENS

Although separation continues to be an issue for preteens, as well as older youngsters and adults, anxieties fall into perspective by virtue of experience. See the Suggested Readings under Death, Divorce, and Illness and Health Care (if you are coping with a hospital stay). Also refer to the following books for adults.

ADULTS

Annie Stories by Doris Brett. New York: Workman Publications, 1988. An innovative way to help parents ease children's fears through storytelling. Addresses the New Baby, Nursery School, Divorce, Death, Hospitalization, etc.

Helping Children Cope with Separation and Loss by Claudia L. Jewett. Boston: Harvard Common Press, 1982. This very helpful book for parents and professionals working with children identifies the stages of separation and loss from the initial reactions to the final "letting go and moving on." Readable, useful, and sensitive.

Learning to Say Goodbye: Starting School and Other Early Childhood Separations by Nancy Balaban. New York: New American Library, A Plume Book, 1987. Expanded from an earlier version for teachers, this is a useful text for early childhood professionals and parents.

Necessary Losses by Judith Viorst. New York: Simon and Schuster, 1986; Fawcett, 1987. A warm and wise book about the many separations we face and cope with throughout the life span—in order to grow. Helpful for adults' understanding of sense of loss and selfhood.

Sex

The era of discussing sex through the medium of "birds and bees" is long past. Today children seem to demand direct and accurate answers to their questions. "*How* direct?" "*How* accurate?" "At what age?" These are the kinds of questions parents and teachers ask themselves.

"Mom . . . how do you *really* make a baby?" Sally's mother looks at her with an expression of caution and wonder. How could this age-old question leave Mom with such a feeling of confusion and inadequacy? And how is it possible that Sally doesn't know more about the reproductive process? Did she sleep through the sex education course at school?

Sally's mother has some alternatives. She can field the query altogether with a "Let's talk about it some other time," give a simplistic answer, expand too much on the topic, or say, "That's a really big and important question, Sally. Tell me what you know and what you're wondering about."

Some time later, Sally's mom has corrected misinformation, answered some of the questions, and put others off for the next heart-to-heart talk. She wants Sally to get more background information from a book with clear but tasteful illustrations and an objective tone, reserving plenty of future time for them to explore together the connections between love, emotion, and sexual urges.

Adults who have difficulty talking with children about sex may find help in books that describe how others have gone about it.

SUGGESTED READING: SEX

VERY YOUNG CHILDREN

How Babies Are Made by Andrew C. Andry and Steven Schepp. Boston: Little, Brown & Co., 1984. First published in 1968, this book seems as fresh and direct today as it did then. Prepared in consultation with the Sex Information and Education Council of the United States and the Child Study Association of America, its somewhat abstract paper-cutout illustrations are clear but tasteful. To be used when a child begins to ask questions. Ages 3 to 7.

Making Babies by Sara B. Stein. New York: Walker & Co., 1984. Photographs of animals as well as human beings illustrate a simple text for young children about the reproductive process. An accompanying text in smaller print is designed to be helpful to parents. Ages 3 to 5.

Where Do Babies Come From? by Margaret Sheffield. New York: Alfred A. Knopf: 1973. Used in England throughout the primary school system, this book is gently and beautifully illustrated by Sheila Bewley. It is also explicit in the most tasteful sense. Ages 3 to 7.

MIDDLE YEARS CHILDREN

Asking About Sex and Growing Up by Joanna Cole. New York: Morrow Junior Books, 1988. The author of this "'question-and-answer book" for boys and girls is a former elementary-school teacher and librarian. Parents and other significant adults should find it a very helpful text as children begin to ask more sophisticated questions. Ages 7 to 9 (and up).

The Stork Didn't Bring Me by Marie-Francine Hebert. Deep-haven, MN: Meadowbrook Press, 1988. A book, guide, and board game for parents who want appealing—but accurate—explanations about sex and birth for their children. Ages 7 to 9.

PRETEENS

Are You There, God? It's Me, Margaret by Judy Blume. New York: Laurel Leaf/Dell Publishing Co., 1986. Margaret worries about the many problems of growing up in this well-known novel. Ages 9 to 12.

Let's Talk About . . . S-E-X by Lorri Foster and Sam Gitchel. Fresno, CA: Planned Parenthood of Central California, 1985. Specifically designated for youngsters ages 9 to 12 and their parents, this interactive guide has space for written responses and a crossword puzzle! The section for preteens is prefaced by one for adults.

Period, rev. ed., by Joann Gardner-Loulan, Bonnie Lopez and Marcia Quackenbush. Volcano, CA: Volcano Press, 1981. Good information in a well-illustrated book that includes children of different backgrounds. Ages 9 to 12.

Understanding AIDS by Ethan A. Lerner. Minneapolis, MN: Lerner Publications, 1987. Accurate facts followed by two hypothetical stories make this new book one of the clearest and best for adults to use with children in talking about today's most dreaded sexually transmitted disease. Ages 9 to 12.

A Very Touchy Subject by Todd Strasser. New York: Laurel Leaf/Dell Publishing Co., 1986. A boy's emerging sexual feelings are the subject of his own story. A novel for mature preteens.

What's Happening to My Body?: For Boys, 2nd rev. ed., by Lynda Madaras. New York: Newmarket Press, 1987. Written with warmth and wisdom, this volume of information talks about growth spurts and reproduction among a wealth of other sexually related topics. The new edition includes information about AIDS. Ages 9 to 12.

What's Happening to My Body?: For Girls, rev. ed., by Lynda Madaras. New York: Newmarket Press, 1987. This rich textbook explains, with understanding of young feelings, the menstrual cycle, breast growth, body changes, and more. The new edition includes information about AIDS. Ages 9 to 12.

ADULTS

The Family Book About Sexuality by Mary S. Calderone and Eric W. Johnson. New York: Bantam Books, 1981. This substantial book is for use by the whole family, be it a "traditional" one or disabled, divorced, single parent, etc.

Raising a Child in a Sexually Permissive World by Sol and Judith Gordon. New York: Simon & Schuster, 1986. A personal and thoughtful book, full of advice and information for adults concerned about today's mores.

What We Told Our Kids About Sex by Betsy A. and Michael H. Weisman. New York: Harcourt Brace Jovanovich, 1987. A concise and factual book that offers a straightforward discussion of human sexuality in a question-and-answer format.

Siblings

All the planning in the world can't condition a child's response to a major event like the birth of a sibling. Children's books to help with feelings of sibling rivalry abound—for good reason.

* * *

Mrs. Anderson's satisfaction over the perfect handling of Jimmy's introduction to baby Jennie has faded in the past week. Everything seemed too ideal when she came home from the hospital. Leaving baby Jennie with her husband, she had greeted Jimmy alone with a big hug and the toy airplane he'd been longing for. Jimmy had looked with seeming interest at the baby, then run off to examine his new plaything.

Days—and many infant feedings and diaper changes later—the Andersons can't help but notice that their son seems angry at them. He says "no" to even the gentlest suggestion, and at his worst, he kicks the floor and screams for no apparent reason. Last night he wet his bed. Jimmy has never hurt Jennie; in fact, he often asks if he can give her a kiss—so he *can't* be jealous . . . can he?

The doorbell rings, and minutes later Mrs. Anderson opens a small package from her best friend. The note reads "I thought you might find this useful—it certainly worked at our house!" The words on the cover of the tiny book say *Nobody Asked ME If I Wanted A Baby Sister.*

Of course rivalry doesn't necessarily cease as baby grows up! There are a number of books available for adults that can put family feelings in perspective and suggest strategies for handling ongoing problems between siblings.

SUGGESTED READING: SIBLINGS

VERY YOUNG CHILDREN

The Berenstain Bears Get in a Fight by Jan & Stan Berenstain. New York: Random House, 1988. Brother and Sister Bear have to find a way to resolve their squabble. Ages 3 to 5.

Betsy's Baby Brother by Gunilla Wolde. New York: Random House, 1982. Betsy's not sure how she feels about a new member of her family. Ages 3 to 5.

Born Two-gether by Jan Brennan. Avon, CT: J & L Books, 1984. Twins present a special kind of sibling relationship. Evocative and charming photographs of different sets of twins help put a range of feelings in perspective in this little volume. Ages toddler to 5.

Devin's New Bed by Sally Freedman. Niles, IL: Albert Whitman & Co., 1986. Although there is no actual sibling involved in this story of Devin giving up his crib for a "real" bed, in many families the reality involves relinquishing one's crib to the new baby. A separation issue as well. Ages 3 to 5.

Hello Baby by Charlotte Doyle. New York: Random House, 1989. Homer's feelings about brand new baby brother Leo make this story perfect for those first weeks with a new sibling. Ages toddler to 5.

I'll Fix Anthony by Judith Viorst. New York: Aladdin Books, 1988. How a little boy feels when he's mad at his older, six-year-old brother. Ages 3 to 5.

It's Not Fair! by Anita Harper. New York: G. P. Putnam's Sons, 1986. Big sister gets mad at all the favoritism shown toward baby brother in this kangaroo family. A fine animal allegory if you don't want to be too explicit about touchy sibling feelings. Ages 3 to 5.

Jenny's Baby Brother by Peter Smith. New York: Viking Press, 1984. Little Pete grows old enough to be a lot more fun than Jenny ever thought he would. Ages 3 to 7.

The Knee Baby by Mary Jarrell. New York: Sunburst/Farrar, Straus, & Giroux, 1988. This classic story about Alan's need for Mommy's lap and his struggle to get her attention has been reissued as a brand-new paperback. A must. Ages toddler to 5.

Let Me Tell You About My Baby by Roslyn Banish. New York: Harper & Row, 1988. Photographs and text tell the story of a little boy's feelings from the end of his mom's pregnancy through her absence in the hospital, and finally, adjustment to little brother's arrival. Ages 3 to 5.

My Mama Needs Me by Mildred Pitts Walter. New York: Lothrop, Lee & Shepard Books, 1983. In this loving black family, Jason learns what it feels like to care for his new baby sister—and to know that his mama needs him. Ages 3 to 7.

The New Baby at Your House by Joanna Cole. New York: William Morrow & Co., 1985. A broad look at children's feelings when a sibling arrives. Ages 5 to 7.

Nobody Asked ME If I Wanted a Baby Sister by Martha Alexander. New York: Dial Books, 1977. Oliver does his best to get rid of baby Bonnie—until he realizes she prefers him to all his friends. Ages 3 to 5.

Peter's Chair by Ezra Jack Keats. New York: Harper Juvenile, 1983. For more than 20 years, this book about Peter's acceptance of baby Susie has brought pleasure and comfort. Ages 3 to 5.

A Place for Ben by Jeanne Titherington. New York: Greenwillow Books, 1987. Ben may have to share his bedroom with little brother Ezra, but he needs his own space. Surprisingly, he needs his brother too! Ages 3 to 5.

Sometimes I'm Jealous by Jane Werner Watson, Rober E. Switzer, M.D., and J. Cotter Hirschberg, M.D. New York: Crown Publishers, 1986. A book for parents and young children that concentrates on putting feelings into words. Ages 3 to 5.

When the New Baby Comes, I'm Moving Out by Martha Alexander. New York: Dial Books, 1979. A fine book to use if you're coping with a youngster who's anticipating the birth of a sibling with hostility, and who needs to know he or she is special. Ages 3 to 5.

MIDDLE YEARS CHILDREN

The One in the Middle Is a Green Kangaroo by Judy Blume. New York: Yearling/Dell Publishing Co., 1982. Freddy is a middle child and thinks that the school play may be the only way he'll ever be recognized for himself. A novel for young readers. Ages 5 to 9.

PRETEENS

Superfudge by Judy Blume. New York: Yearling/Dell Publishing Co., 1981. A novel about coping with a younger brother who's so wild he's not even called by his real name. Ages 9 to 12.

ADULTS

He Hit Me First: When Brothers and Sisters Fight by Louise Bates Ames with Carol Chase Haber. New York: Dembner Books, 1983. Sibling rivalry seen as a natural phenomenon, but one for which adults need to develop strategies. From the Gesell Institute of Human Development.

The Sibling Bond by Stephen P. Bank and Michael D. Kahn. New York: Basic Books, Inc., 1982. A probing exploration of the sibling relationships affecting all our lives.

Sibling Rivalry by Seymour V. Reit. New York: Ballantine Books, 1988. Sponsored by the Bank Street College of Education, this book gives perspective on the roots of rivalry, discusses birth order, and gives a heap of practical advice as well. Includes help for problems involving stepchildren and twins.

Siblings Without Rivalry by Adele Faber and Elaine Mazlish. New York: Avon Books, 1988. Empathy and suggestions abound in this book written by mothers of sibling children.

Sisters and Brothers by Judy Dunn. Cambridge, MA: Harvard University Press, 1985. A book from "The Developing Child Series," this work gracefully incorporates research studies with plain language. Common problems covered in a serious way.

5

DEALING WITH
A TOUGH TOPIC:
Pieces of a Puzzle

Imagine that ongoing communication about one of the
life issues or problems discussed in this book is a kind of
jigsaw puzzle and that there are several puzzle pieces
that need to fit together in order to make the picture
whole. Let's take the topic of *sex*, as an example, and look
at some of the "pieces" needed to complete the picture of
you, your child, or your pupil comfortably discussing or
exploring ways to make an appropriate and helpful conversation possible.

Puzzle Piece One:
The Individual Family's Values and Beliefs

Even though parents don't always agree, each family has its own style and specific feelings about various subjects. You may believe strongly that the way you learned about sex worked for you and will work for your child, even though experts disagree. Perhaps you want to give your child a more gradual introduction to the subject, or you remember a particular moment when your mother or father seemed to give the "perfect" explanation. Some parents may feel that sex should be taught in school through sex education classes, while others feel it should only be talked about at home. Some teachers may endeavor to answer questions simply, while others make it a rule to refer all personal inquiries to the family. Certainly the emotional linking of love and sexual urges is an essential and individual issue for each family.

These are considerations for adults to struggle with, although most experts recommend direct answers to children's questions, with appropriate information supplied according to the child's developmental stage.

Puzzle Piece Two:
The Child's Questions and Behavior

One of the biggest clues concerning what to say and when to talk to your child about sexual issues will come directly from him. Watching his actions, listening to her questions, you will know that a response is needed.

In Chapter 2, Listening and Responding to Children, you have some suggestions about picking up on clues. Books listed in the section on *sex* in Chapter 4 will give you a wealth of suggestions about how to approach sexual issues.

Puzzle Piece Three:
The Child's Age and Stage of Development

If you have not had an opportunity to study child development, Chapter 3 will give you some indication about what kinds of information children can digest at various ages and stages. Birth is most often the first aspect of sex we talk about with children, an obvious (physically) and often natural introduction. But it's also useful to remember that all children are sexual beings in the sense that they can feel pleasure from their bodies as soon as they come into the world. Born with the sucking reflex, they receive instant bodily gratification through nursing at bottle or breast. For further reading on how children develop emotionally, physically, and intellectually, here are some suggestions:

The Learning Child by Dorothy Cohen. New York: Schocken Books, Inc., 1988. About toddlers to 12-year-olds.

The Magic Years by Selma Fraiberg. New York: Charles Scribner's Sons, 1984. About toddlers to 6-year-olds.

Raising A Confident Child by Joanne Oppenheimer, Betty Boegehold and Barbara Brenner. New York: Pantheon Books, Inc., 1985. About infants to 12-year-olds.

Your Baby and Child from Birth to Age Five by Penelope Leach. New York: Alfred A. Knopf, 1978.

Your Child from Five to Ten by Arnold Gesell, Frances I. Ilg and Louise B. Ames. New York: Harper & Row, 1977.

Puzzle Piece Four:
Accurate Information

Children are receiving information all the time. They learn by listening to and participating in conversation, exposure to the media, and through books. If what they hear, see, or read is beyond their capacity to comprehend, they will carry around a load of misinformation.

Parents and teachers, as adult thinkers with years of experience to boot, are obviously a lot more knowledge-able than their children and pupils. There may be, how-ever, significant gaps in *their* understandings. The adult who can say to a child "I really don't know the answer to your question. Let's try to find out about it together." is an adult who will be turned to again and again.

Little children want only the clearest and simplest answers to their questions. A three-year-old's "Where do babies come from, Daddy?" answered by "They grow inside the mommy's tummy until they are big enough to be born." may be all that's called for.

It's a different story for older children, who are work-ing in progressively more complex ways to understand the messages received from their environment. Middle years children often muster courage to question the adults in their lives after reading novels written with their period of development specifically in mind. (Wit-ness the popularity of Judy Blume's *Are You There God? It's Me, Margaret.* See Suggested Reading: Sex.)

But we shouldn't be fooled into thinking that all the facts have fallen into perfect place! A young mother with whom I recently spoke confided that the sex education video shown when she was ten to her fourth-grade class at school left her terrified and confused. I asked if there had been a chance for discussion afterward or an invitation to speak to the school psychologist on an individual basis. "No." What a deplorable situation! Information *must* be accompanied by reassurance. As you decide it's time to discuss homosexuality with your preteen son because you're frightened by the growing number of AIDS victims, a book such as *What's Happening to My Body?: For Boys* (See Suggested Reading: Sex) can provide accurate, factual understandings of homosexuality and information on the transmission of the AIDS virus, which you and your son can read separately or together. (There is an equally good edition of the above for girls, and many other helpful books on sensitive sexual issues.) Reading together can be the point of "talking departure."

Traditionally, intimate sexual issues come up at home, and if a teacher is faced with a sex education opportunity, there is nothing wrong with a simple answer, followed by "Have you spoken to your parent(s) about these questions?" This is as direct, honest, and appropriate as any graphic reply. You, the teacher, need to know the family's views before going further. If the child indicates difficulty in making contact with mother and/or father, you may be able to assist in getting them together. If not, referral to the school counselor is a good alternative.

Puzzle Piece Five:
Facing an Issue at Home and in School

The beloved principal of an elementary school recently died of AIDS. Unlike some big-city schools, his was a close-knit community. He was a man of stature and compassion whose sexual orientation was never a matter for speculation. The progress of the disease he contracted was rapid and—unlike many AIDS cases—not terribly obvious.

The principal's death caused widespread mourning among teachers and families, and the school itself was kept running by dedicated staff members who organized to cover administrative responsibilities and kept in close contact with parents during the painful period of transition.

The first letter received by parents from the transitional administration informed them that the principal had died of pneumonia, the reason also given to the children. But this explanation caused a rush of concern among the younger students who were aware of a severe case of pneumonia recently contracted by a child within the school. If their principal had died of pneumonia, then maybe children would start to die of pneumonia!

The next letter written to parents covered ways to help them talk with their children about death, in line with what teachers were discussing in classrooms. Then, abruptly, the principal's family decided to speak openly about AIDS as the cause of his death, and the school had a decision to make. Should they convey this information to all members of the school community—including parents and children—or simply continue to mourn the loss of their admired leader?

Deciding to respect the family's decision to bring the actual reason for death into the open, the school staff drafted yet another letter to parents. The staff also began a program of AIDS education with the children, one appropriate to their ages and to their strong feelings about a man they both looked up to and loved.

In working through this trauma, the entire school took

part together in the NAMES project (squares of material carrying deceased persons' names, put together in memory of AIDS victims), completing 250 squares. Every child and adult had a chance to remember and to mourn the principal's passing. A celebratory service was held at which everyone who wished to had the opportunity to speak. They sang together, and they cried.

In this complex and painful incident, the issues surrounding AIDS were faced and grappled with. Both children and adults were able to express their anger, fear, and mourning during the process and to experience resolution through the culminating events.

Puzzle Piece Six:
Books as Tools for Discussion

There is no easy "how to" for parents and teachers seeking help in talking with children about sex or any other tough topic. The warmth and comfort underlying the relationship between an adult and a child is the irreplaceable foundation for conversation.

We face, however, formidable odds as we try to converse meaningfully with our youngsters. At a time in our society when single-parent families are rapidly approaching a figure close to 50 percent, statistics also show that 80 percent of families with both parents in the out-of-home work force will soon be a fact of life. Time with our children is precious indeed. These numbers, in turn, put teachers—as role models—under added pressure.

Television, videos, and films have significant impact on many of us. More statistics indicate that the average young child watches approximately 25 hours of television per week, and some of this exposure can be both scary and confusing. Just imagine a three-year-old's reaction to a "hot" episode on an afternoon "soap" or an older child's response to a rape/murder reported on the evening news.

Surrounded as we are by visual images, the point of this puzzle piece—and the point of this book—is to help us remember the tremendous power of the written word. It's easy to forget that reading and writing used to be our major avenues of communication. Books are, among their other joys, immensely powerful vehicles for discussion.

6

Literacy
and Learning
to Read

One of my favorite books for parents who are anxious about whether or not their children will learn to read is called *Reading Begins at Home* by Dorothy Butler and Marie Clay. It defines reading in a broad but sensible way as "the transfer of meaning from one mind to another through the medium of written language." Stressing the importance of the home environment as fertile ground for the emergence of literacy, the authors report on a significant study.

A fascinating project was carried out by Dr. Margaret Clark in Glasgow in 1976. It has special interest for our purposes because it concentrates on the lives of thirty-two children all of whom could read by the time they entered school at five. These children came from different backgrounds, from the very wealthy, to the very poor. But they all came from families where books were read and stories were told. One little boy, whose father was an unskilled laborer, was the youngest in a family of seven. His older brothers and sisters had all learned to read easily, too. Questioning revealed that the father of the family, although he had left school at fourteen, loved fairy stories and had always told them to his children. Both he and his wife enjoyed reading, and had taken the children regularly to the public library. Although money was short, the family owned books. No one had tried to teach the youngest child to read at this early age; surrounded by books and people who read for pleasure, he had learned.*

During the years that I was a primary grades teacher, I began to notice that by middle to late first grade, I could mentally divide my class into three approximately even groups: children who were spontaneous early readers, children who were "on the road" to reading, and children whom I determined to watch carefully to see if they "just weren't ready yet" or would perhaps need some remediation.

In my classroom, children had a wide selection of books to peruse and to share in conference with their teacher or with each other. There were many kinds of print in view, all used in meaningful ways—as signs, labels, attendance cards, or charts of children's experiences. I read to the class every day. Children were also exposed to phonic games. These I felt to be much more

*Reading Begins at Home by Dorothy Butler and Marie Clay (Heinemann Educational Books), p. 9.

effective than the mandated workbooks (which we also tried to pretend were a kind of game!). Writing was plentiful, evolving slowly from an individual child's name on a picture, to one (or a few) letters standing for words, to whole words and sentences. We worked on spelling in an informal manner, and this seemed to free the children to write longer and more involved stories.

By the end of the second grade, children were proud of their complex, edited stories and legible handwriting, delighting in reading their own "published" books to fellow classmates and any visitors who would listen. All of the children were exposed to the same environment, and I was able to observe them over a two-year period because the school policy was to stay with primary-grade youngsters for two years running. As a persistent pattern, I continued to notice the three-part division among my students in mid-first grade, followed by a dramatic "thinning out" of the third I had been worried about by the end of second grade.

Recent research shows that, in fact, I was being a little more vigilant than necessary. Approximately 10 percent of an average first-grade class can benefit from active intervention in the early reading process in the form of one-to-one, teacher-to-child, extra attention. Ten percent of *that* 10 percent will need continued support to compensate for a learning disability. This research suggests that the richest possible environment in terms of books, stories, and opportunities to write without constant correction, both at home and in school, will allow for the emergence of literacy among most of our youngsters.

For those children who have continuing difficulty in learning to read and write, help is usually available through programs in our public schools. Special education teachers have the skills and techniques necessary for helping those who need remediation, while parents can help most of all by encouraging their children and having confidence in them. Self-esteem emerges in an atmosphere where less anxiety means more success.

In my travels around the United States during the past few years, parents have sometimes said to me: "But *I* can't read! How can you expect me to help my child become a reader by reading him a story, or to make a problem easier to talk about by reading a book on a tough topic if I, the adult, don't have the skills to do it?" There are twenty million adults in this country who are functionally illiterate, but there are programs to help them. If you are reading this book and know a person who can't read or write, put him or her in touch with an organization that can help, such as the Literacy Volunteers of America or the Coalition for Literacy. (The Coalition's toll-free national literacy hotline number is 1-800-228-8813, or in Nebraska only 1-800-228-3225.)

Whether or not you are an avid reader yourself, you can value stories and enjoy the written word in its many printed or handwritten forms. Having appropriate books available, making trips to the library, telling children stories, and respecting their scribbles, are all ways to lead children to literacy. Once there, they will have effective skills, not only to enhance their enjoyment and competence but also to help with the tough topics that lie ahead on the inevitable road of "growing up."

INDEX

Parents and teachers, as collaborative
  partners, 2
Parents Anonymous, 24
Piaget, Jean, 6
  theory of "open education," 9
Pregnancy, 31, 75

Return to normal pleasures, ix
"Rules of thumb," 20

Separation, 58-59
Sex, 14, 15, 31, 63, 72, 73, 74, 78
  experimentation with, 21
  talked about at home, 73
  taught in classrooms, 73, 75-76
Sexual abuse, 24
Sibling rivalry, 15, 66

Siblings, 66-67
Spock, Dr. Benjamin, 8
Sputnik, 8

Teachers, as researchers, 9
  goals of, for children, 1
  important influences of, x, 2, 10, 78
Teachers and parents, as collaborative
  partners, 2
Television, 78, 79
Traditional values, 9

U.S. Census Bureau, 44

Videos, 78

Worry, by parents, 4